Century Bank bases its strength in the ability to understand the needs of the people within the communities it serves. Our fundamentals and roots remain the same in satisfying our customers with a quality of service that creates value in banking with Century. This community commitment makes us extremely proud to sponsor this unique pictorial history on the city of Lynn which also commemorates the Society's 100th anniversary.

Our commitment to the people and businesses of Lynn is supported by our ongoing endeavor to enhance the quality of life through our professional work, public service, and charitable giving. In fulfilling these responsibilities, we constantly strive to maintain the highest degree of integrity.

We dedicate this album to the citizens of Lynn and the Lynn Historical Society for all their dedication and pride in keeping the city's past alive for future generations to enjoy. It is only through our past experiences that we can learn and plan for the future.

Century Bank

People investing in people.

2 State Street
Lynn, MA 01901
1-800-442-1959

Member
FDIC

Allston/Brighton, Beverly, Boston's North End, Braintree, Burlington, Cambridge, Everett, Lynn, Malden, Medford, Peabody, Salem, Somerville, Wollaston (Quincy)

EQUAL HOUSING
LENDER

John W. Hutchinson was the last of the large reform-oriented family singing group that had lived at the base of Lynn's High Rock since the late 1830s. In 1904, Hutchinson gave High Rock to the city with funds to build a stone tower at its summit. He stands here at about that time, on the steps his family built in 1881 leading up the hill. Hutchinson died in 1908.

In order for "the humblest citizen to enjoy in common ownership the privileges of beach and ocean that nature has so generously favored our city with," construction of Lynn Shore Drive began in 1904. It was finished three years later with the completion of the Metropolitan District Commission bathhouse. An underground tunnel once connected the bathhouse to the beach across the street. Photograph courtesy Metropolitan District Commission

We are pleased to have a part in the presentation of the

The Lynn Album II
A PICTORIAL HISTORY

and to help commemorate the Lynn Historical Society,
a vital member of our community, that leaves its legacy of our past
with the expectation that the future be as meaningful.
The courage and hardiness of our ancestors continues today.

Daily Evening Item
HASTINGS AND SONS PUBLISHING COMPANY

Chronicling daily news of Lynn
and its surrounding communities
since December 8, 1877

End Page Photographs:

Cover Photographs
Top To Bottom:
Members of the E.C. Brown, R.O. Brown, B.E. Flamer and L. Middleton families, Easter, early 1970s
Market Street, December 1953
Carla Mary Morris preparing for her English High Prom, 1962
General Electric Co. workers, 1980s

Background Photograph
Lynn Heritage State Park Mural

Inside Front Cover
Clockwise:
G.E. River Works, December 1949
Aerial view, City Hall Square, about 1931
Great fire of November 28, 1981
Graduating class of Pickering Junior High, 1964
Dynamiting ice, Lynn Harbor, about 1930
High Rock Tower, 1990s
Market Square, about 1935
Livermore/Peterson cookout, Rand Street, 1953
Surf sailing, King's Beach, Spring 1988
Livermore/Peterson Christmas, Rand Street, 1952
Center photograph: Lynn Woods, about 1990

Inside Back Cover
Clockwise:
S. O. Breed & Co. Lumberyard, Beach & Broad streets, 1889
Washington & Broad streets, Great fire of November 28, 1981
Jail & Bail Day, May 23, 1988
Central Square, about 1935
Dyer-Fitzgibbons Gas Station, Western Avenue & Chestnut Street, about 1940s
St. Stephens Tennis Court, September 1889
Intersection Summer & Commercial Streets, 1976
Graduating class of Pickering Junior High School of 1987
Lynn English High School Stage Crew, 1952
Center Photograph: Lynn Woods, about 1990

Published in the United States of America 1996
by the Lynn Historical Society
125 Green St.
Lynn, MA 01902

Book design by Jerry Day
Cover design and end pages by Marcia Ciro
All photos, unless otherwise credited, are in the collection of the Lynn Historical Society.

Library of Congress Catalog Card Number 96-076791
ISBN 1-882162-12-9 (hardcover)

Foreword

Dear Friends:

The Lynn Historical Society celebrates its one hundredth anniversary in 1997. To kick off this event, the society is publishing *The Lynn Album II: A Pictorial History*. Picking up where *The Lynn Album* left off, this second volume chronicles the city's last century. The society is fortunate to have an outstanding collection of photographs that document the rich history of modern Lynn—its triumphs, its tragedies, and its greatest asset, its people. This collection was supplemented by photographs from many friends, who came forth with images that recall other memorable events and people but that are not yet among the views Lynn Historical preserves. We are grateful to have been able to include them, and we hope you enjoy *The Lynn Album II*.

Kenneth C. Turino
Director

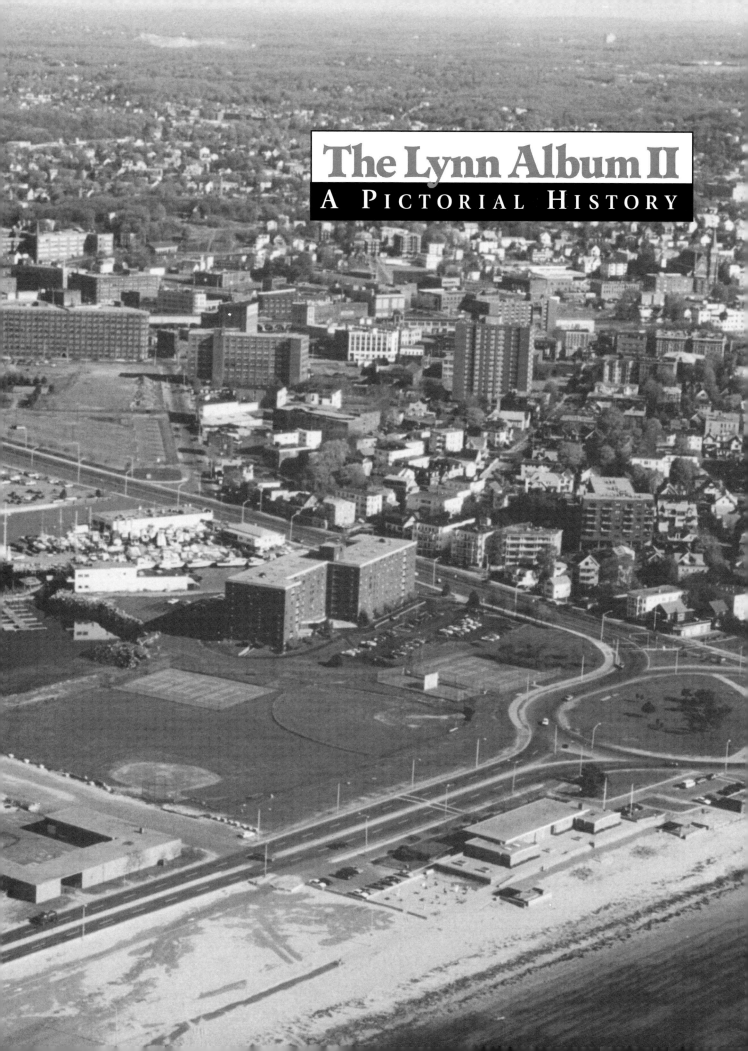

The Lynn Album II
A PICTORIAL HISTORY

Workers building Buchanan Bridge across Glenmere Pond posed for a photographer in 1921 or 1922. The bridge replaced the Floating Bridge, which had carried people, carriages, and even circus parades across the pond for more than a century but was no longer safe by the end of World War I. Photograph courtesy Philip Trapasso.

Table of Contents

The pier of the Lynn Yacht Club in 1897. The club was home to several championship yachts in its early days and recently celebrated its 125th anniversary.

Acknowledgments

*T*he *Lynn Album II* has been in the planning stages since the publication of the Lynn Historical Society's first photographic history, *The Lynn Album*, in 1990. The project has entailed collecting photographs from the 1930s to the present to supplement the historical society's own collection. Many individuals and organizations have contributed their time, effort, and photographs to this project.

The Board of Directors under President William Conway gave its full support to this publication; Conway himself lent several images and helped identify many others. The society was fortunate to have historian and author Kathryn Grover research and write the text and work with us on photo selection. This is the first comprehensive history of Lynn in this century, and the majority of Grover's work was based on original research largely in the historical society's collection that had never been published. Another person who deserves special thanks is Vincent O'Brien, the former managing editor of the *Lynn Daily Evening Item*, who read every draft of the book manuscript and used his extensive knowledge of the city's recent past to enrich many of the photograph captions. The staff of the society, particularly librarian/archivist Diane Shephard and administrative assistant Fay Greenleaf, researched and verified information; they along with curator Heather Johnson and museum educator Pearl Brown proofed the manuscript. Photographic assistant Don Livermore spent hours locating and filing photographs. Lois Basilio, Jeanne Stella, and volunteers Peggy Dee, Jean Kelley, Yefim Romanosky, and Al Weber all offered assistance.

Numerous people supplied information as well as photographs. Librarian Judy Johnson and photographer Walter Hoey from the *Daily Evening Item* generously gave of their time, as did community editor Suzanne Hamil and sports editor Bob Keaney of the *Sunday Post*. The Lynn Public Library was kind enough to lend photographs and assisted with research. Thanks especially go to chief librarian Joan Reynolds and reference librarian Nadine Mitchell. John Cronin of the *Boston Herald* lent photographs, as did Aaron Schmidt of the Boston Public Library. Sean Fischer of the MDC Archives was of great help with photographic research. Local 201 IUE president Jeff Crosby and aircraft executive board member Jeff Francis provided information on Lynn's labor history that could not be documented through other sources, as did Virginia Barton and Phyllis Brown Dykes-Hector with respect to the history of Lynn's African American population.

As ever the society is fortunate to have photographer Hal Cohen of Lancer Studio in Lynn copy photographs. Marcia Ciro designed the cover and end pages. Jerry Day designed and produced the book.

This publication would not have been possible without the sponsorship of Century Bank & Trust Company (George Swansburg, president) and the *Daily Evening Item* (Brian Thayer, publisher, Molly Evans, marketing director, and Kevin Kelley, advertising director). This project is supported in part by the Lynn Cultural Council, a local agency, and the Massachusetts Cultural Council, a state agency, and the collaborative Scholar in Residence program of the Massachusetts Foundation for the Humanities and the Bay State Historical League.

Looking southeast from High Rock toward the Nahant peninsula, this view shows Lynn in 1898, nine years after the great fire. To the left, new brick factory buildings arose on the site of what once had been a largely wooden district of more than 150 shoe manufacturing shops and related "shoe and leather houses." By 1915 eight large, new brick structures would be erected in the area as well.

Chapter 1

Portrait of a City:
Lynn at the Turn of the Century

A century ago, Lynn was a city that had risen up from a devastating fire to face a future of almost unparalleled promise. Despite the fact that the fire of 1889 had nearly swept its thriving shoe and leather industry completely away, Lynn reigned eight years later as the premier shoe manufacturing city in a region that produced more than 60 percent of the nation's shoes. It was the second-largest manufacturing center for morocco leather in the country. And in 1893 shoe production had begun a steady rise that would continue until the First World War: the city's shoeworkers produced 15 million pairs, chiefly of women's shoes, a year.

In 1897 the prosperity of Lynn's other major industry, electrical machinery, was only just beginning to be realized. By 1897 the five-year-old General Electric Company, created from the merger of Lynn's Thomson-Houston Company and the Edison General Electric Company of Schenectady, New York, was already one of the largest in the industry. It had pioneered the development of arc and incandescent lighting, of turbines and generators to produce electrical power, and of motors to power electrical railways. Lynn had served as a showcase of the company's

electric street lighting prowess since 1890, and for decades afterward municipal officials from all over the country would visit "the best lighted city in the world." For as many decades, Lynn people referred affectionately to General Electric's West Lynn Works as "the Lights."

There were other signs of the city's robust condition. Lynn Harbor, though shallow, was ranked eighth in the country for barge traffic; more than one million dollars worth of raw materials

The fire of 1889 left an eerie skeletal char covering acres of the central city. Having begun in a wooden glove-kid factory on Almont Street, it destroyed 334 buildings before it was extinguished. Crowds surveyed the ruins at the corner of Washington and Munroe streets.

13

Noon time at the West Lynn Works of General Electric Company on Federal Street, 1905; the Weber Leather Company tannery is at right. The West Lynn Works was GE's original plant in Lynn; its second plant, River Works, opened in 1893. Together the plants employed four thousand people in 1900, paid out $2.5 million in wages, and produced $5 million worth of products. GE was still a distant second to the shoe manufacturing, supplies, and machinery industries, which together employed more than twenty thousand people and manufactured goods valued at $30 million.

(principally coal, sand, lumber, and hides) and finished products (principally shoes) passed in and out of the harbor each year. The city had just finished building a new post office in 1897, had organized its historical society, and had received the bequest that would allow it to begin construction of a new public library. Since 1898 two newspapers vied for the attention of city dwellers, the *Lynn Evening News* having started up in competition against the twenty-three-year-old *Lynn Daily Evening Item*. By 1900 the sense of recovery was complete. "With the exception of here and there an uncovered spot of ground," city officials noted, "there is little to remind us of that fiery ordeal of 1889, and the final summing up of its results will show them to be an unquestioned good."

In 1897 Lynn was just beginning the ethnic transformation that had already changed textile communities along Massachusetts's Merrimack Valley. At the last federal census, in 1890, 31 percent of Lynn's population aged ten and older (and thus potentially in the work force) was foreign-born, and another 17 percent had been born in this country to foreign-born parents. In Lowell, by contrast, 55 percent of the population was foreign-born in 1890, and 20 percent were native-born children of foreign-born parents. The huge looms and other machines of mass-produced textiles were concentrated in large factories that drew immi-

grants by the thousands to the textile towns. But unlike Philadelphia's shoe industry, which had been organized into centralized sweat shops, Lynn shoemaking had for years depended upon labor dispersed over a wide region. Before industrialization, Lynn manufacturers had sent shoes to women in dozens of towns along the North Shore and in

On July 23, 1898, city officials and workers laid the cornerstone for a new public library on North Common Street. Four years earlier Lynner Elizabeth Shute had provided money for its construction, and by 1898 Lynn contractors Shea and Donnelly were at work carving the columns for the structure, built of stone from the company's Brickyard limestone yard and designed by Boston architect George A. Moore. The building was dedicated on April 4, 1900, and remains in use as the city library.

At the turn of the century, A. E. Little and Company was preeminent among those Lynn shoe manufacturers who rested comfortably on the high quality of its products. The company's Sorosis shoe was a high-grade "staple" sold all over the country and in Europe; it exemplified local manufacturers' slogan, "Lynn Shoes are Best Made Shoes." A. E. Little encouraged company loyalty by establishing the Sorosis Annex for its female employees, some of whom posed about 1900 for this scrapbook photograph. Company officials declared that the club was "but one of several means the makers of Sorosis shoes have employed to put into practice the theory that the obligation of an employer to his employees does not end with mere payment of wages for labor done."

New Hampshire and Maine for binding and had sent them out again to men in the same places for lasting; according to historian Allen Dawley, "pre-factory shoe manufacturers assembled the largest labor force of any industry in New England." And by the time the myriad trades involved in making shoes were consolidated under factory roofs, the putting-out system had created a pool of skilled labor in the countryside. Until the turn of the century, Lynn shoe shops tended to be populated largely by Lynn natives and former northern New Englanders, as well as by smaller numbers of Irish and English Canadian workers, groups that had emigrated before and immediately after the Civil War. In 1895 less than 24 percent of the city's shoe workers were foreign-born, though more than 60 percent of its leather workers were.

Lynn's foreign-born people in 1890 were on the whole a more homogeneous group than were Lowell's immigrants. Nearly 88 percent of all Lynn's 8,174 immigrants aged ten and older had been born in Great Britain, English Canada, or Ireland; in Lowell slightly less than 64 percent of foreign-born residents had been born in these English-speaking countries. By contrast, only 6 percent of Lynn's immigrants had been born in French Canada, while fully 33 percent of Lowell's had been. By the turn of the century, there were only a few churches in Lynn—two Swedish parishes (one

evangelical and the other Lutheran), one "French" church (St. Jean Baptiste), one Jewish congregation (Avas Hachin), and one Pentecostal church—that appear to have been created by and for immigrants. There was also a smattering of churches that had grown out of the holiness movement of the previous century and catered largely to poor people, including the Salvation Army and its offshoot Volunteers of America, but most Lynners worshiped in the churches of old-line congregations. There were thirteen Methodist or Methodist Episcopal churches (including one African Methodist Episcopal church), four "orthodox" Congregational churches (so called to distinguish them from more liberal outgrowths, the Unitarians and Universalists, who had three churches in Lynn), seven Baptist churches, three Roman Catholic churches older than St. Jean Baptiste, two Quaker congregations, and two Episcopal churches.

Reflecting the organization of the turn-of-the-century labor movement into different trades, fully twenty unions and scores of other lodges represented and protected the city's shoe and leather workers. Lynners also formed themselves into nearly seventy clubs representing neighborhoods, political wards, schools, and causes: on February 16, 1898, a day after the explosion of the U.S. battleship *Maine* in Havana harbor killed Lynn's Charles Johnson and 265 other officers and men,

six young men organized themselves into the Lynn True Blues, who dressed themselves in the style of Theodore Roosevelt's Rough Riders, marched in parades throughout the region, and even offered amateur theatricals. Lynners had watched the *Abby Deering* sail out of the harbor the year before, carrying city people seeking to make their fortunes in the gold rush to the Klondike, and now in April 1898 thousands gathered in Central Square to watch young men leave the city to serve in the Spanish-American War.

But by 1900 the war was over, the troops had returned, and Lynn had marked its fiftieth anniversary as a city with a week-long celebration in May. "Lynn is having a happy time this week, celebrating her 50th Anniversary," the Boston *Record* noted on the occasion. "Fortunately, it comes just when everybody is prosperous down there. The factories and mills are running full. Lynn is a lively town, but it makes a great difference with its appearance how the wages are coming out daily."

The festivities seemed to demonstrate that Lynn "has all the other places under its feet, in a figurative sense, as a usual thing," noted the perhaps envious *Times* of Brockton, another shoemaking city. Lynn had long thought of itself as a city of shoeworkers whose skill produced shoes admired everywhere. "Our city is not a Newport or a Saratoga to which wealth is BROUGHT but a city

where wealth is MADE BY LABOR," wrote shoeworker Ellen Wetherell in 1903. ". . .The Shoe Industry has been, and is Lynn's life." Census statistics seemed to support this view: in 1890 35 percent of the male population above the age of ten and 38 percent of all working-age women were employed in shoe and leather industry jobs in the city. In a 1901 issue of the trade journal *Shoe Retailer*, Martin E. Welch of the local shoe manufacturing firm Welch and Landregan declared that Lynn children "were born in the business of shoemaking":

> That they should one day or another join the ranks of the shoemakers of the city was with them a matter of course from their childhood. . . . The children on the street practically know nothing but shoes, and let a boy at the age 12 or 14 start to work and ninety-nine times out of a hundred you will find that it is within the walls of a shoe factory. He meets his companions and they ask him what he is doing. The chances are that he will tell them that he is inking edges, cementing channels or something of a like nature, with the result that the other youth goes home to his family and asks for a chance to go to work the same as his neighbor.

At the semicentennial celebration, Lynn Historical Society president Benjamin N. Johnson expressed the hope that Lynn would not only remain supreme in shoe manufacture but would

be driven into the worker." Johnson termed this notion part of a "larger view" that had stimulated efforts to legislate a shorter work week and paid vacations, as well as to set aside "public reservations in wood and park and along the sea" such as Lynn Woods, and, soon enough, Lynn Shore Drive and the city's beaches.

Yet amid such certainty and hope for the future, characteristic not only of Lynn but of Progressive-era thinking in general, ran the suggestion that prosperity in Lynn would not continue to be as easily achieved as it seemed to have been in the eleven years since the great fire. Even as the shoe and leather shops were running at full schedules, most Lynn shoe workers were not fully employed. In 1890 32 percent of males and 38 percent of females in Lynn's labor force were unemployed for

also be the first to "achieve a rational, healthy and permanent understanding" between shoe workers and shoe shop owners. Part of this understanding, Johnson argued, would include the "determination that the insensate hurry of the machine shall not

In 1890, when Lynn's coastline was completely taken up by private residential, commercial, and industrial property owners, citizens began to work together to reestablish public access to the shore. In 1892 the new Lynn Park Commission purchased land from Nahant Street to Beach Street to create Oceanside Park and later added land from Red Rock to the Swampscott border. By 1898, when this photograph was taken, Lynn Beach was a popular recreation area with a photograph gallery. Photograph courtesy Harvey Robinson.

part of the year, compared to 12 percent of men and 11 percent of women in Lowell. These figures reflect the seasonality of the shoe trade and suggest strongly that Lynn workers were not earning enough to live on comfortably year round. And within a few years, workers in both the shoe and electrical industries would begin to react angrily to changes brought about in part by "the insensate hurry of the machine." Workers at General Electric's two Lynn factories chafed under the impact of time-motion efficiency studies. And both style and technological changes would lessen the need for skilled shoe workers, upon whose reputation Lynn's idea of itself greatly depended. As craft skills became less important, craft-oriented unions were less effective in representing workers' interests. Both the shoe industry and, later, General Electric would become embroiled in complicated and bitter struggles to shift the basis of the labor movement from trade to industrial unions, and local labor leaders in both

industries were at the forefront of efforts to create for each "one big union."

Yet in 1900 this struggle was scarcely visible on the horizon. Lynn was about to embark upon nearly two decades of spiraling prosperity, which in turn stimulated a population explosion that would remake the city both physically and ethnically. The invention of gasoline-powered vehicles coupled with this industrial and commercial vigor to propel a transportation revolution that also changed profoundly the way the city would look—and would begin slowly to break down how the city was organized. Cohesive and often geographically defined neighborhoods, long a feature of life in Lynn, would begin to weaken as the automobile demanded its own kinds of spaces and allowed Lynners to live easily elsewhere. But this change too was not apparent to anyone in 1900, when the newly rebuilt city believed itself about to become stronger than ever.

At the turn of the century, Central Square was a bustling interchange soon to become even more active. This view, looking northwest from the Lynn Item building, shows the tracks of the Boston and Maine Railroad and the apparatus of its increasingly dangerous grade crossings; here also are the tracks of the Bay State (later Eastern Massachusetts) Street Railway Company, one of two trolley lines serving the city. The tower of the A. E. Little shoe shop, bearing the Sorosis shoe slogan, is just right of center in the background. Thousands of shoe workers poured out of Little's and other factories and into lunch rooms and restaurants in Central Square after every shift; here Harry Huntt had opened two restaurants, one so heavily patronized by shoe workers that it was nicknamed "Crispin's Congress." Another Central Square eatery, Earl's Restaurant, had been popular with shoe workers since its opening in 1863 but was razed within the decade to make room for the elevation of the Boston and Maine's tracks.

In 1900 most of Lynn's ten-footers—so called because most of these early shoe shops measured ten feet square—had been put to other uses. As early as 1855, local historian David N. Johnson noted, most had seen service again as "hen-houses or coal-pens, or were moved and joined to some house to make a snug little kitchen"; many others became clubhouses. In 1899 the office of the storage warehouse Tewksbury and Caldwell and of justice of the peace M. F. Delnow occupied this ten-footer on South Street.

Since 1804 Glenmere Pond had been traversed by the city's famed 511-foot Floating Bridge; one Lynner called the pontoon bridge "virtually a raft moored at the ends." Boys often sat on the rails of the bridge and waited for a heavy wagon to sink the structure, when they would run back and forth through water above their ankles. The span was notorious for frightening circus elephants, who would rather plunge into the pond and swim across or take the long way through the woods than cross it. J. C. Vickery photographed the well-used bridge in January 1901.

In 1900 Lynn's principal shoe manufacturers gathered for a meeting in Wolfeboro, New Hampshire. In charge of the city's best known and oldest firms, these men for the most part represented traditional Yankee culture. As late as 1911 thirty of the 103 shoe shops in the city were controlled by families that had established them in the 1800s, and they produced two-thirds of the city's annual output of shoes. Shown here are John Nickerson, Harry Emery, Samuel Musso, William Pierce, Henry Morse, Thomas Collier, Jr., and George H. Batchelder.

Ice cutting on Flax Pond by ice dealers Z. J. Chase and Sons, after 1892. Saugus River ice had been shipped from Lynn harbor to the East Indies before the Civil War, but as the coastal ice trade shifted to the north Lynn's many ponds produced ice for the local trade. Once the ice was sawn almost completely through, workers finished the cut, and still others used hooked poles to guide the four-by-six-foot cakes to the ice house. Ice was harvested in Lynn until 1930 or 1931, when the last harvest took place at Beede's ice house on Flax Pond. By that time electric refrigerators had become widely available and affordable.

Even though a Lynn newspaper noted that there were twenty different kinds of automobiles in use or being built in Lynn by the fall of 1899, horses were still the dominant mode of transport in the city by the turn of the century. Lynn Fire Department's equipment depended upon horses; above, the horses pulling Engine No. 4 waited outside a fire at the Smith House on Howard Street in 1903. A nearly full milk wagon and other delivery wagons stood near a Pleasant Street railroad crossing, below right, on November 3, 1906. And city confectioner Ira T. Nador stood proudly next to Nador's Ice Cream and Egg Nog cart, drawn by a single pony and touted as "the smallest business team in the world."

Bonfires, like this one set to be lit on Broadway on the Fourth of July in 1902, were common throughout the city to mark momentous occasions. The 1900 semi-centennial included a bonfire at High Rock, a conflagration of barrels and boxes city householders and storekeepers had contributed to celebrate the event. As the fire raged, the Eighth Regiment band played popular and patriotic tunes to the accompaniment of cowbells and horns played by the attending crowd. High Rock had been the site of many "stupendous bonfires" in Lynn's past. Photograph courtesy Harvey Robinson.

By 1900 Lydia E. Pinkham Medicine Company had been without its founder at the helm for seventeen years, but it continued to be a thriving manufacturer of the company's famed Vegetable Compound well past the Second World War.

Lynn at the turn of the century was a city of clubs. In this 1895 photograph the Old Boys of Ward 4 posed at their second annual outing in Nahant, where member John W. Hutchinson entertained them with songs, other members recited old school poems, and the men enjoyed a traditional clam chowder lunch complete with crackers, pickles, cake, pies, apples, coffee, and after-dinner cigars. Businessman Henry Breed formed the group in 1893 from "the old boys of the ward," none of whom was younger than sixty years old. The aged, white-bearded men formed themselves into a club as the old order they represented was passing: a new generation of clean-shaven, efficiency-minded men born after the Civil War was soon to take control of industry in Lynn as elsewhere.

Civic spirit was high in Lynn; in this view Jeannette Carlton Burnham Fleet wears a dress fashioned from copies of the Lynn Daily Evening Item.

Lynn Historical Society was one of the largest local historical societies in Massachusetts by 1910, but it lacked its own headquarters and met in the rooms of the Oxford Club and Lynn Gas and Electric during its first sixteen years. The 1910 bequest of Charles F. Pierce enabled the society to buy the Wooldredge House at 125 Green Street, built by carpenters Daniel Hyde and William H. Mills for their own use in 1836. The society began to fit the rooms up with historical exhibits and to occupy the building in 1913.

At the turn of the century Sluice Pond was a popular recreational spot in the city that had also long been put to commercial uses. A trolley car barn and several ice houses occupied its shoreline, as did two boathouses that rented canoes and rowboats to people on outings. Boat liveries and ice houses remained on Sluice Pond up to about 1930.

To provide entertainment for Lynn's large working-class population, at least five new theaters opened in Lynn between 1897 and 1915. The Olympia, opened in 1908 next door to Bennie's Lunch on Washington Street, offered vaudeville and films and was Lynn's largest theater; former Item *managing editor Vincent O'Brien recalls how Geoffrey Whelan stood on the Olympia's darkened stage and "talked" for the movies in the days when film was silent. In 1910 the Central Square (later the Capitol) Theatre opened on Union Street and offered a regular live program of "high class vaudeville," including touring singers, dancers, animal acts, and acrobats; the Strand (later the Warner) opened in 1915 as Lynn's first "luxury" theater, complete with a large orchestra and an elaborate set depicting Mount Vesuvius and the Bay of Naples.*

Chapter 2

The March of Improvement:
Lynn before World War I

In 1899, two years after Lynn Historical Society was created, member Charles Buffum announced a plan to place one of Lynn's ten-footers on the Common. The society had scoured the city for one of the old shoe shops and had at last secured the donation of the shop of Amos Tapley, one of the city's first shoemakers. The shop by that time had been moved down Mall Street from its original location on North Common Street to the backyard of the Lye house, where it had most recently been occupied by the family hens. At that time at least seventy ten-footers then remained in Lynn. But Tapley's shop, despite its rotted sills, broken windows, and loosened clapboards and shingles, was a relic with genuine historical significance, as Buffum saw it; in the words of one Boston newspaper, the historical society felt the shop should be saved to "preserve the memory of the days of the old back yard shoe shop, where the grandfathers of some of us made a pair of shoes before breakfast each morning."

Having no property of its own until 1913, the historical society proposed placing the shop on the small Common, "better known as the Park," Buffum said, "nearly opposite the armory and in full view of the new Public Library building." Buffum promised to add "a little paint and a few new boards" to make the structure presentable, to install concrete walks to and around the building, and to see to it that flowers were planted in beds between the walkways and the shop. A brass rail was to surround the structure, the newspaper noted, so as to keep "strangers from picking off the shingles for souvenirs."

But Buffum's plan ran counter to the way other people saw the Common. Even the newspaper agreed that the Tapley shop would be "a sorrowful comparison" to the "handsome new Library Building." Building Inspector Herbert C. Bayrd was hotly opposed to the plan. "I'd resign before I'd permit them to put the old shanty on the Common," he told the Boston reporters. "In the first place I don't believe any private concern, no matter what its character, has a right to permanently take possession of any part of our Common, and to put up an old shoe shop there would be a desecration. If they want to preserve the memory of the old shop," Bayrd asked, "why don't they get a picture of one and hang it up in the new Public Library building?"

Clearly, Lynn in 1900 was a city in which the soft tread of nostalgia was drowned out by what city newspapers over and over again termed "the march of improvement." Between 1890 and 1900 both the historical society and various city clubs had been formed in the interests of hanging on to Lynn's past, but between the turn of the century and the Depression a large number of structures that modern Americans view as historic and irreplaceable fell as the city rushed headlong into its most prosperous time.

Despite a dip just before World War I and mounting evidence of a declining shoe industry, between 1900 and 1920 the city's economy was healthier than it had ever been. Between 1900 and 1925 population rose 63 percent, from 63,500 to

Lynn's phenomenal growth after the turn of the century came at the expense of much of the older city. In 1907 these two nineteenth-century Federal-style homes, the Richard Cutts and Shaw houses, were torn down to create Haddington Place, which by 1915 housed eleven families in four multifamily dwellings.

103,000. The largest five-year increase the city ever experienced took place between 1905 and 1910, from 77,042 to 89,336 people; between 1915 and 1916 alone more than 6,600 persons became Lynners and pushed city population above 100,000 for the first time in history. To accommodate this influx, the city needed new housing, stores, and places of entertainment; to accommodate this commercial growth and the dynamic pace of industrial advance, the city needed business blocks and factories. In 1912 the *Board of Trade Journal* noted that "more than $2,000,000 worth of additional city valuation is represented in the new buildings which are now under construction in Lynn, and indications point toward the establishment of a record, especially for large apartment houses and factory construction." A year earlier the *Lynn Item* had observed, "That Lynn has been almost completely rebuilt, made over, re-established and modernized within the short space of 40 years is a sentiment of observant Lynners, whether native-born or not. Not much of old-time Lynn remains."

The city's stunning growth changed the city in two ways. First, housing new people and businesses tended to make the city more crowded and more vertical. Factories were built taller, and triple-deckers and apartment buildings occupied the same lots that single-family homes had earlier. Vacant lots were filled up, and many houses did double-duty as corner stores. Slightly later and more gradually, the development of gasoline-powered vehicles, as well

as of some larger industries, tended to push the city outward, to change it from a vertical one to a horizontal one. Cars needed their own vast spaces, and both their huge popularity and the need to park ever greater numbers of them eventually pushed much of Lynn's commercial life to its edges and many of its people to the suburbs.

Before the First World War, however, growing population, healthy retail and industrial economies, and the automobile all spelled progress. Some of old Lynn remained: a few early nineteenth-century houses were not razed, and many vendors and small businesses used horses into the 1950s. Yet most gave way, and in their place arose vast numbers of new rental units, new commercial blocks, new theaters, bowling alleys, pool halls, grocery stores, and restaurants; it was a city full of life. One former shoe worker recalled, "There were more people going out to eat in Central Square in Lynn than any place in Boston during a busy time. There were twenty places to eat along Central Square. There were plenty of us there, plenty of people there at noontime. It was good, it was a busy place, Lynn, it was one of the busiest places there was on the North Shore."

Construction workers prepared a site on Silsbee Street for the new market of J. B. Blood Company in 1916. Opened in 1881 with just fifty pounds of granulated sugar and ten gallons of kerosene, the market and bakery chain began to expand in 1907 as population soared. Blood's second market opened on Union Street that year, but by 1916 the increasing popularity of the automobile compelled the company to buy land on Silsbee Street to create a parking lot as well as a new fireproof building. By the Second World War, J. B. Blood had two markets, its Beehive Bakery, ten Beehive Bakery stores, and sixty trucks delivering Beehive baked goods, Blood's own coffee, tea, and baked beans, and other groceries house to house. The apartment house at the rear of the view must have been a fairly new addition to the street at that time.

At around the turn of the century, shoe factory workers in shirtwaists leave one of the downtown factories for their lunch break. By 1915 four of every ten shoe workers was a woman, and the Lynn stitchers' local was one of the most active female-run locals in the nation. Photograph courtesy Library of Congress.

Building for Prosperity

By 1911 the shoe industry in Lynn reached its peak. More than 103 shoe manufacturing companies were in business in the city. They employed twelve thousand people to produce fifteen million pairs of shoes valued at thirty-three million dollars. One hundred other firms were allied leather companies or service firms, and General Electric was just about to buy acres of land, then occupied by wooden factories and one frame house, in order to expand its original plant. The city also began to buy and raze houses in West Lynn in the hope that other factories would build there.

Between 1903 and 1912, local historian Richard L. Vitale has noted, seventy-seven factories were built in Lynn, or about eight a year. Among them were the massive factories erected by Edward E. Strout's Lynn Realty Company between 1903 and 1915. Lynn Realty was the successor of Lynn Building Trust, organized in 1905 "to attract industry to Lynn and establish the city as a major manufacturing center." With designs by local architect Henry W. Rogers, the company erected eight brick buildings along Broad and Washington Streets and in the process created eight hundred thousand square feet of floor space, fully occupied by shoe firms through the First World War. Lynn Realty's Vamp building (so named because its floor plan resembles a shoe vamp), built in 1903 and expanded in 1907, was claimed to be the largest structure devoted to shoe manufacturing in the world.

The original plant of General Electric in Lynn, at Western Avenue and Fairchild Street, was in the midst of expansion when this photograph was taken in 1910.

The Burdett, George E. Coffin, and P. J. Harney shoe companies all occupied Lynn Realty Trust's Building #6 in 1919. Through the First World War Lynn Realty's eight factory buildings were fully occupied. Building #6 was at 278-88 Broad Street at Marshall's Wharf, where the companies received their raw materials and shipped their finished products. Hides from South America, California, Mexico, and India destined for Lynn first came into the Port of Boston and were reloaded onto lighter coasting schooners for shipment to Lynn; likewise, Lynn shoes were taken by barge to Boston, much better connected by rail to the rest of the country. Through the 1910s, contracts between shoe shops and Lynn and Boston wharves made it cheaper to ship shoes by barge than by rail.

While shoreline land east of the Nahant peninsula had been developed into a scenic boulevard in 1910, downtown Lynn extended to the waterline and beyond it with wharves, coal companies, and triple-deckers at lower Washington Street on the west side. The Bay State Street Railway's power house is shown in this view, taken from Nahant Beach.

Well into the middle of the twentieth century, factories and homes shared the same Lynn streets. Opposite the seven-story brick J. J. Grover shoe factory (right) on Buffum Street in 1910 were the boarding houses of Mrs. Margaret J. Barnett, Honore Bourget, Sabina Green, and Balbina McGuire; at 41 Buffum the National, probably an apartment hotel, may also have boarded shoe factory workers.

Factories, most of them four to eight stories high and housing shoe firms of various sorts, filled nearly every available downtown space by 1910.

Between 1899 and 1909, according to historian Keith Melder, more than seven thousand new workers joined others in these shoe factories to bring total employment to eighteen thousand. These workers needed low-cost housing, groceries, and entertainment, and city entrepreneurs quickly began to buy up vacant lots and old homes to serve these needs. The 150-year-old Neal house in Woodend was razed for a "modern block" in 1904; the city fire department's first engine house was demolished "for a block" in 1907; the 200-year-old Breed House at Summer and Orchard Streets gave way to a "modern block" in 1908; and both the Stephen Smith estate on Market Street and a century-old house and store at the corner of Federal Street and Western Avenue were torn down for the same purpose in 1909. Earlier business blocks judged too small or too primitive for the modern age were razed for new ones, including the flatiron Dickson block and the structure at 33 Market Square, then one of the city's oldest commercial buildings and the site of Security Trust Company's new building in 1914.

Many more buildings came down to create housing. Between 1900 and 1925, Melder has pointed out, 4,251 structures were built for housing;

many of them arose close to the city's industrial center, thus preserving in large part the walking city Lynn had been in the nineteenth century. "On streets formerly characterized by wide spaces between dwellings and ample back yards, vacant land was crowded with new housing," Melder observed. "Many courts and terraces were added within residential blocks by the solid massing of multifamily buildings. Thus many newcomers to Lynn could occupy housing within a mile or two of the shoe factories." The Lynn Park Commission

The density of triple-decker neighborhoods is clear in this snapshot of the back yards of several of them. Lynn was a city in transition, as the horse-drawn cart racing down the street at rear makes clear.

By 1908 C. Sargent Bird's drug store had occupied the busy corner of Federal Street and Western Avenue since 1875. The structure, built in about 1803 as a tavern for stage drivers on the turnpike, had also housed several grocery stores in the nineteenth century. In 1909 the structure was razed, the newspaper reported, "to make way for the March of Progress."

houses in which they lived. The overwhelming majority of shoe factory and probably of other industrial workers were renters, and making space for them to live in involved some traditional strategies and some new ones.

First, boarding and lodging houses, many of them run by women, became far more common. Between 1897 and 1910 their number as city directories recorded them more than doubled, increasing from 63 to 175; by 1914 there were 226. Most were within half a mile of Central Square. A 1911 U.S. Senate Immigration Commission study revealed that while a "considerable proportion" of shoemakers' wives were looking for regular employment outside the home in 1909, "a much larger proportion of the wives" took in boarders or lodgers.

noted in 1911 that eight tenement houses "packed like sardines" and housing 377 people had been occupied by an orchard and a grocery store only six years earlier. Historian Naomi Rosenblum has noted that the expansive back yard of the Anthony House at 166 Washington Street became a three-decker enclave called Quincy Terrace, while other Washington Street homes were razed or moved for new multiple-family dwellings. The Marion Street home of famed local merchant Billy Gray was torn down for "modern tenements" in 1908, the 1846 Pevear House on Essex Street was razed the same year for "four of the most modern apartment houses in Essex County," and the estate of Caroline S. Kimball at Ocean and Bassett streets was broken up for apartment buildings in 1911. The comparatively ancient Minute Man Tavern in West Lynn, built in 1667, was taken down for apartment houses, and even such venerated sites as the Clubroom Tree of Ward 5 and the Broad Street cemetery—full of "Quaker bones," as the newspaper put it—were bulldozed for apartments and business blocks.

Building for People
Lynn was a city of single-family homes into the 1890s. Yet many of these homes were rented to workers, not owned by them, and one 1915 sample of shoe factory workers listed in the city directory found that only 18 percent actually owned the

Between 1900 and 1902 Washington, D.C., photographer Frances Benjamin Johnston came to Lynn to photograph living and working conditions among the city's women shoe workers. Some of Johnston's photographs appeared as illustrations in the 1903 book The Woman Who Toils; Being the Experience of Two Gentlewomen as Factory Girls. *The book was written by Mrs. John Van Vorst and Marie Van Vorst, women unaccustomed to factory work who decided to enter the shoe shops as a way of portraying realistically working conditions for women. Photograph courtesy Library of Congress.*

Of the 463 households investigators surveyed in 1909, one-third kept boarders or lodgers, and the tendency to do so was nearly universal among Lithuanians in Lynn. In addition, more than eight of every ten Polish households in the city housed others for extra money, while, at the other end of the scale, less than 15 percent of the city's Armenians and English-speaking people did. One sample of shoe factory workers taken from the 1915 city directory found that 30 percent lived in boarding houses (which fed as well as housed them), rooming or lodging houses, or in rooms in other people's homes. Very few of these boarders and lodgers were listed among city residents in the 1910 or 1920 directories, suggesting that they were not permanent residents. As early as 1884 one shoe worker complained to the *Lynn Item* that the city was overrun with an "unorganized floating population" who came for shoe factory work when business was good and returned to their farms when it was slack; by 1903 this "floating population" was made up principally of younger shoe factory workers who traveled between eastern Massachusetts's shoe towns—Lynn, Boston, Haverhill, Salem, and Brockton—as well as from "Italy and Maine," as one capitalist put it. An estimated minimum of 30 percent of the work force changed jobs every year. "The frequency with which the eye meets the sign

Many of the city's single-family homes were reconfigured after the turn of the century to accommodate burgeoning growth. Many were divided into multi-family units, while others, including this home at the corner of Ashton Square and Chestnut Street, was revamped to house a street-level corner store.

'Rooms to let' convinces a visitor that the population of Lynn must be in a state of constant coming and going," the 1915 U.S. Department of Labor study *The Boot and Shoe Industry in Massachusetts as a Vocation for Women* reported. "Those who come are more than those [who] go." A year earlier, the local Board of Health had made note of the fact that most of the least expensive lodging houses offered no place to bathe, a clear violation of sanitary codes. But public health officials felt they should be allowed to remain open nonetheless, for to "close them . . . especially during the winter would turn into the streets many men who for the small sum of 10 cents or 15 cents are now privileged to sleep indoors."

One of the new techniques Lynners seized upon to house shoe factory and other laborers was the triple-decker, an innovation that housed three families in the space single families had generally occupied up until the 1890s. The triple-decker was a comparatively late arrival in Lynn; by 1900, when nearly all of Boston's triple-deckers had been erected, only eighty-four of an estimated fifteen hundred triple-deckers in Lynn by 1925 had been built. By 1902, and particularly between 1905 and 1915, triple-deckers became abundant in Lynn; more than one hundred were

In 1912 the City Hall Studio photographed the northwest corner of Franklin and Endicott streets as workers sandwiched a triple-decker onto a small lot beside one just built and a much earlier residence. Like many Lynn triple-deckers, the structures were flat-roofed and had two-story front porches.

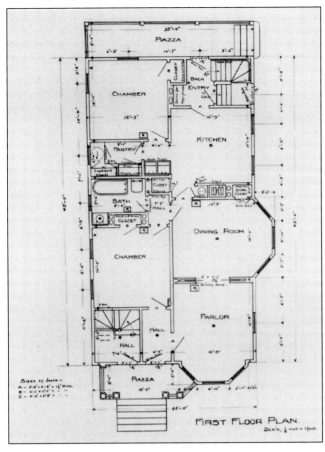

At the end of 1906 Lynn architect Dana A. Sanborn prepared plans for a triple-decker for local clothing merchant Samuel Goodman. The plan on the upper two floors mimicked that of the first, and in many triple-deckers dining rooms and parlors sometimes served as extra bedrooms.

put in place each year between 1909 and 1912, and in some years half of all dwellings built in the city were of this type. Triple-deckers in Massachusetts were built in several different styles—some with hipped roofs, some with front porches on all three stories, some with back porches—but Lynn's tended to feature flat roofs and porches on either all three levels or on just the first story. Triple-deckers were usually freestanding on all or on three sides and had back yards, like houses, but in Lynn as in other industrial cities they were often built so close to each other that ventilation, light levels, and outdoor space made them more like apartment houses. Only a few triple-deckers were owned by families who lived in them. By the mid-1910s most triple-deckers were valued at about four thousand dollars, well beyond the

ability of most shoeworkers to afford, and at that time the cost of living was rising at a far faster clip than shoeworkers' wages. Most triple-deckers were developed as rental property investments by realty companies or private entrepreneurs, and in Lynn many were designed by just four firms—Henry W. Rogers, who had designed Lynn Realty's industrial buildings; Dana A. Sanborn; M. F. Burke, and Edwin Earp and Son.

Another housing novelty of twentieth-century Lynn was the apartment house, a somewhat later development than the triple-decker and originally referred to as an "apartment hotel." Between 1914 and 1925 the number of apartment buildings listed in Lynn directories increased from thirty-two to sixty-one, and on the whole they housed many more families in far smaller spaces; in 1928 one building for thirty families took the space of the single-family Bacheller house on Broad Street. Perhaps because they seemed so unlike the homes most had grown up in or later lived in, apartments were manifestly less popular among Lynn workers; the 1915 directory sample of shoe factory workers found that only slightly more than 2 percent lived in them.

Patrick B. Magrane, an Irish immigrant turned Market Street department store owner and Lynn real estate investor, erected these two apartment houses at the corner of South Common and Elm streets. Few Lynn workers lived in apartments before the war, but they may have turned toward them more often afterward as the pace of triple-decker construction slowed. In the inflationary years after World War I, Magrane also opened a grocery store at the former Boscobel Hotel at the end of Lynn Common to offer food at low prices; when fish prices skyrocketed, the Boston American opened an emergency "bargain" fish market in Olympia Square as well.

To some extent, building the city up to house many more people involved an outward growth as well, and just as historic properties could be devalued in such a climate so too could open space. "In a number of directions Lynn is spreading out, and reclaiming farm and marsh and pasture lands," the *Item* noted in late November of 1912. "Within a few years, new residential sections have sprung up, many new streets have been laid out, and scores of homes have been built where desolation existed." Walter E. Jewett was then creating a housing development known as East Lynn Park, and a new boulevard called Ocean View Avenue, on Alden Waitt's old farmland along Eastern Avenue; homes had begun to be built on the leveled pasture land in the Highlands section in about 1900. At Fairmount Park, a housing development established in 1880 by the Lynn Workingmen's Aid Association to encourage shoe workers to buy land and build homes, a "second boom" around 1902 stimulated the creation of

The J. P. Conley grocery store was at the corner of High Rock and Acorn streets in the rapidly developing, and overwhelmingly Irish American, Highlands section of the city. The clean-aproned man at center is owner Joseph Conley, who also operated a larger store and bakery at Rock Avenue and Hollingsworth Street. The store's meat department offered roast beef for a mere fourteen cents and legs of lamb for twenty-two cents per pound; on the floor, orders packaged and put in baskets awaited home delivery.

Making low-cost goods available to workers became the chief goal of many Lynn retailers. Kennedy's and Gately's clothing stores in downtown Lynn used a by-then rare vacant lot at the corner of Liberty and Sutton streets in 1910 to advertise the easy terms on which clothing could be had; by suggesting it "pays to walk" to Kennedy's, the store owners implied the prices were right.

another set of house lots. The rural estates of Michael Fenton on Boston Street and of Richard Fay were divided into cottage lots in 1913 and 1916; on the Fenton lands developers announced plans "to erect homes that will average $3000 in value, and sell them to the public on the easy payment plan."

But on the whole, the majority of workers lived very near where they worked, as they had the century before, and the electric trolleys kept even farther-flung workers within minutes of the heart of the city. There and along trolley lines developed grocery stores, restaurants, clothing stores, and numerous places offering entertainment to workers and their families in the few hours left for leisure in a work week of forty-eight to sixty hours. In 1915 there were more than twice as many pool rooms (one of them run by Joe Milo, an Italian immigrant whose shoeshine parlor has been a famed Lynn landmark into the present), bowling alleys, and theaters in the city as had been there in 1897, as well as various other businesses that catered to a working-class population—nearly sixty laundries (more than half of them run by Chinese immigrants), seven

Salem retail buyer W. T. Grant opened the first of what became a nationwide chain of discount department stores in Lynn in 1906. The first store occupied the ground floor of what was then the new YMCA building on the corner of Market and Tremont streets. One early ad promised that nothing cost more than a quarter in a store "of revelation values."

The many workers living in lodging houses needed places to eat, and the Ideal Dining Room at the corner of Western Avenue and Center Street offered "home cooking" by the day, week, or meal as well as fare "at all hours." For a week's worth of meals in 1909, as the hand-painted window notices indicated, women paid three dollars and men fifty cents more. That the dining room was busy is also clear: a paper sign reading "waitress wanted" had been affixed to the window.

pawn brokers, twenty junk dealers, and numerous low-cost clothing and variety stores. The vitality of Lynn and its large laboring population probably convinced W. T. Grant to move from his buyer's job for Salem retailer Almy, Bigelow and Washburn in 1906 to begin his own 25-cent store on Market Street in Lynn, on the site of what was then the city's new YMCA. In Salem, he was often struck by the fact that the store "always ran out of 25 cent articles"; at his store in Lynn before the First World War, Grant later recalled, "why, we could completely dress a woman and send her out on the street with 25-cent items from the store." By 1946 Grant had built a nation-wide chain of five hundred stores.

With so many workers in lodging houses, Lynn also needed low-cost restaurants. In 1897 the city directory listed five eating houses and forty-nine restaurants; a decade later there were four "lunchrooms" and eighty-four restaurants; and in 1910 one hun-

dred restaurants were listed, far more than exist in Lynn today. There were at least six Chinese, six Greek, three Armenian, and one Italian restaurants, and by then Harry Huntt had four eateries in the city; he added five more in later years.

Two diners shared the corner of Sutton Street and Central Avenue in 1910, not far from the headquarters of the Lynn Police Department. By the telegraph pole is a White House Café, almost certainly built by Lynn's Ephraim Hamel at his small Wheeler Street factory. At right is the Union Lunch, and between them the Lynn Theatre posted a sign advertising its production of Uncle Tom's Cabin, *a popular stage play throughout the country for years after the book was published in 1852.*

There were also many restaurateurs who catered to workers on the night shift, a common feature of Lynn shoe factories since about 1900. Among them was Durkee's Restaurant and Lunch Room, "open day and night" at 44 Munroe; the "night lunch" run by E. F. Fitzgerald on Union Street; and five "lunch wagons" and "lunch carts." These lunch wagons were the predecessors of diners, of which Lynn's Capitol Diner of 1928 is the preeminent local example, and some of them were manufactured in Lynn as early as 1892 by Ephraim L. Hamel, a Canadian native who had moved to Lynn as a boy and had worked as a dinker, or leather cutter. In 1891 Hamel began to run a night lunch from his house at 49 Wheeler Street, and the next year he began to build White House Café Lunch Wagons under an arrangement with a Worcester manufacturer. The Hamel family built the tiny, sixteen-foot-long White House Cafés at a factory near their home until 1910, and at least two operated in greater Lynn. The working-class nature of many of the city's eating places was abundantly clear, some of them even advertising themselves as "strictly a union house," such as MacKenzie's Lunch on Blake Street, or including the word "union" in their names. Wyman's Union Lunch on Munroe Street was open all night and advertised "tables for

Although he shared the patent and production for White House Cafés with Worcester lunch wagon builder Thomas Buckley, Ephraim Hamel probably built the White House Café 439 that stood on Bass Point Road in Nahant. The first lunch wagons to feature windows on all sides, the White House Cafés were always painted white and, like Number 439, were often embellished with portraits etched into their frosted-glass windows. Photograph courtesy Larry Cultrera.

women" in recognition of the weight Lynn's women carried in shoe manufacturing. Equally popular, especially for its chopped ham and western sandwiches, was Johnny Joyce's tiny Ireson Street restaurant; the street was later renamed for Joyce, a veteran city councillor.

Theaters also did a thriving business in Lynn before the First World War. Where three had operated in the city in 1897, eight entertained Lynners in 1915. Among them was the Auditorium, which opened in 1905 opposite Lasters Hall on Andrew Street and featured a resident company that put on new plays every week. Actors who later became famous on Broadway or in Hollywood, including Edna Mae Oliver, Charles Bickford, and Lester Lonergan, began their careers at the Auditorium. Lynn's Billy "Square Deal" Grady went on to become a theatrical agent for tenor Enrico Caruso and movie star W. C. Fields and then the longtime casting director for Metro-Goldwyn-

The Peoples Lunch Room occupied the northwest corner of Blake and Mulberry streets in 1910, close to the A. E. Little, W. H. Myron, and Faunce and Spinney shoe factories. The former home next door was now a boarding house with furnished rooms to let and dining rooms; a chalkboard leaning against the front door promised that the proprietors kept a "neat house," perhaps in an appeal for female tenants.

Mayer studio. Oscar winners Walter Brennan, Estelle Parsons (daughter and granddaughter of well-known city attorneys), and Jack Albertson were all Lynn natives who went on to film and television stardom.

Many Lynn theaters featured vaudeville, concerts, and motion pictures for a nickel or a dime admission fee. The generally thriving atmosphere in Lynn was enhanced just before the First World War when General Electric installed experimental lights and standards in Central Square and along Market, Munroe, Oxford, and Union streets; the city's streets were comparatively brilliant at night, and the city began to proclaim its great "white ways." After the war the lighting program proceeded apace, and by the late 1920s even tiny Pinkie's Diner in Wyoma Square had changed its name to White Way Grille.

Industrial Success—and Strife

That Lynn attracted so many newcomers can only be explained by its enormous need for labor after 1890. Shoe industry productivity climbed steadily through the turn of the century, culminating in 1909 when eighteen thousand people were at work in Lynn shoe shops and all Massachusetts shoe manufacturers produced 118 million pairs. Five hundred new shoe firms, most of them short-lived, established themselves in Lynn between 1900 and 1915. Yet running beneath this prosperity were several trends that would transform shoemaking in Lynn, all of them set in motion by style changes in the industry.

First, Massachusetts in general, and Lynn in particular, were beginning to lose preeminence in shoe manufacturing as the industry turned toward cheaper, more fashionable shoes made in outlying areas. Even a revival after the First World War could not stem the long-term decline. In 1879 Massachusetts shoe shops had made two of every three pairs of shoes produced in the United States. But by 1919 production had dropped by a third, and two of every three pairs of shoes were made outside the state. The state's slide from the top only grew steeper over the next decade. In Lynn, signs that its hegemony in shoe manufacture was threatened had begun to appear by 1909. Over the next five years the value of shoes produced in Lynn dropped by

$1.7 million, and the huge growth in employment in shoe factories up to that year began to reverse itself. By 1914 more than two thousand workers who had been working in 1909 were no longer employed in the shoe shops. In the smaller shoe town of Brockton, however, value of product rose, and over the next two decades competition from that city and other Massachusetts shoe centers grew intense. Lynn was still the country's top shoe center in 1914, but within five years Haverhill and New York City would eclipse it. After the war and into the 1920s competition would also appear from shoes made in Europe and in northern New England, where land and labor were cheaper to acquire and taxes were not so burdensome.

Second, Lynn laborers, whose organization at the turn of the century one historian has described as "chaotic," grew much more assertive as market changes seemed to compel manufacturers to sustain profits by reducing wages. Lynn had always been on the front lines of the labor movement. In 1860, as the shoe industry mechanized, unskilled labor began to be hired to run machines that performed the jobs skilled workers had heretofore done, and the consequent wage reduction stimulated the nation's largest strike to that date. Lynn shoeworkers formed a local chapter of the shoemakers' Knights of St. Crispin a year after it was founded and affiliated with the rising Knights of Labor in large numbers as soon as it reorganized as an industrial union in 1879. Lynn shoe workers had organized themselves in thirty-four Knights of Labor affiliates by the next decade.

After 1895, however, many Lynn workers had begun to feel the Knights leadership was too conservative and began to join the newly organized Boot and Shoe Workers Union, which lured them away with promises to bargain for an eight-hour work day and wage equality for women workers. In Lynn, women had always been a big part of the shoe factory labor force—in fact the city employed more women in its shoe shops than any other shoe manufacturing center in the state—but they were paid half the wages men received. Nearly 40 percent of the total shoe factory labor force was female, and, according to one 1915 government survey, a higher percentage of these women were married than in any other boot and shoe town. That

The Boot and Shoe Workers Union stamp was plastered onto the side of George H. Allen's box factory on Broad Street at the foot of Market Street in 1910. By that time, the BSWU "union label" had far less influence over both owners and workers in Lynn shoe factories as the United Shoe Workers rapidly gained power and influence in the years after the disappointing 1903 strike.

of the largely female stitchers' union, then affiliated with the Boot and Shoe Workers, went on strike. In the end, the stitchers formed a new local within the Knights of Labor, and the cutters affiliated with the rising star of the American Federation of Labor, an agglomeration of unions organized on the old principle of segregation by craft. When the strike was over, more Boot and Shoe locals left the union, eventually formed the Lynn Joint Shoe Council, and ultimately reconstituted themselves as the United Shoe Workers of America in 1909. By 1913 the United Shoe Workers had more than eleven thousand members, though the much-weakened Boot and Shoe Workers Union continued to claim the loyalty of other Lynn shoeworkers.

Wetherell, who wrote a book about the 1903 strike for "Trades Unions, Wage Workers, Men and Women, Heads of Families, Mothers of Children, and the Public in General," laid part of the blame for the strike at the feet of the cutters for harboring a "narrow minded policy of holding themselves aloof from the other crafts to which they are naturally linked by a common industry." Wetherell also

fully a third of the female work force was married suggests the real necessity for two incomes in an industry where employment was never a steady, year-round proposition.

By 1900 even the strong Lasters Union had agreed to affiliate with the Boot and Shoe Workers, and the skilled workers in Local 3662 of the Cutters Assembly agreed to do so if the union could earn the agreement of twelve of the city's shoe shops to carry the Boot and Shoe Workers stamp. As shoeworker Ellen Wetherell put it, the competition between the Knights and the new union ended in an "embroglio" that year as the Knights, claiming that "stamp factories" paid cutters less than union wages, reneged on their promise. Cutters began to walk off their jobs, and when the Boot and Shoe Workers began to hire replacements to fill agreed-upon contracts with their companies, the cutters and the members

Few photographs are known to exist documenting the many strikes that troubled Lynn's shoe industry from the 1890s until the Second World War, but this front-page story from the Lynn Item of January 21, 1903, gives some sense of the hostility of the 1903 strike. When Lynn cutters and then stitchers struck the Walter Tuttle factory over a wage cut, the union brought cutters and stitchers in from out of town. Support for the workers was so high that Lynn restaurants and boardinghouses refused to serve the out-of-town "scabs." Ultimately, the union set up a stitching room, brought in food as well as workers from out of town, and lodged the workers on cots in its hall.

believed that most Lynn workers were largely concerned only with the "few cents more or less per day it [the union] might bring into or take out of our pockets" rather than with the principles behind the combination of laborers into unions. In her view, a labor organization oriented to the needs of all workers in an industry rather than to skilled crafts was "a golden canopy under which a happy, intelligent and cultured people shall develop, making a natural combine of WEALTH MAKERS instead of an artificial combine of WEALTH GETTERS." In the end, as mechanization made many skilled trades obsolete in the shoe and other industries, the appeal of a union that considered all industrial workers equal increased. It culminated in the creation of the Congress of Industrial Organizations in the 1930s, a movement in which Lynn shoeworkers were again central figures.

The third undercurrent in the shoe industry was the gradual shift of the industry from the hands of Lynn's Yankee establishment to that of new, and largely Jewish, immigrants. Unlike the textile indus-

try, meeting the capital requirements of shoe industry ownership was a relatively easy affair. First, shoe shops used far smaller machines, needed smaller amounts of space, and tended to be smaller ventures: 63 percent of all Lynn manufacturing establishments in 1920 employed twenty or fewer wage earners, and only one factory (assuredly General Electric by that time) employed more than one thousand workers; in the nearby textile city of Lawrence, nine factories employed more than a thousand workers each, or fully 74 percent of all the city's wage earners. According to historian Stephen Mostow, the shoe trade was so diffused among small firms in 1910 that not even the two most profitable shops controlled 10 percent of the city's total shoe trade.

Moreover, in the shoe industry both machinery and space were generally rented, not purchased. Lynn Realty Company and other property firms leased space in their large buildings to numerous shoe shops, and the United Shoe Machinery Corporation, formed in 1899 from the merger of the nation's five largest shoe machinery companies, leased machines for a royalty payment on each pair of shoes produced. United Shoe Machinery Corporation lessees were not permitted to use any other kind of equipment nor to have it serviced by any other company, and the company made lease terms easy to meet in order to have as many of its machines in production as possible. Thus it became possible for people with little capital to become shop owners. The city's new Russian Jewish residents, many of whom had been shoemakers or worked in needle trades before emigrating, went to work in the shoe shops and did piece work at home to save money to rent space and equipment; others went into the smaller lines of work in the industry, such as "findings" (the bows, buckles, straps, and other shoe ornaments and supplies) or collecting scrap leather, "dinking"

The factory of leather remnant firm Jacobson and Jacobs stood on the southeast corner of Charles and Commercial streets in 1909. Founded in about 1901 on Alley Street by Isaac Jacobson and Louis Jacobs, Jewish shoemakers who had emigrated to Lynn in the mid-1890s, the company occupied an old wooden shop. By 1915 one-third of the city's employed Jewish population was working in shoe factories, and one-half worked in trades such as scrap leather that were dependent on the industry. By 1927 Jewish entrepreneurs owned twenty-five dinking firms in Lynn, all of them using remnants to fashion unblemished pieces of leather for infants' shoes.

As the city ranked at the top in the manufacture of women's shoes, Lynn was a logical choice as the site of the Industrial Shoe and Leather Exhibit, which took place in this period at the Lynn Realty Trust Building #5 at the corner of Broad and Washington streets.

or flattening it, and cutting it into smaller pieces for children's shoes or shoe parts for resale. Joseph Musinsky, a shoe repairer in Kiev before he emigrated to Lynn in 1890, worked as a laster for a few years in numerous factories before he began to buy up sample, returned, and damaged shoes from Lynn shops. After fixing the shoes at home, he sold them to friends, and within seven years he had saved enough to begin a wholesale factory seconds store downtown in which his three sons later worked.

Changes in consumer preferences also favored the work of smaller shops. In the 1800s, when skirts reached to the ground and people walked frequently, what mattered in women's shoes was durability and fit; women generally bought two pairs a year, one in the spring and one in the fall. But after 1900 numerous technological improvements stimulated an unprecedented concern for style in the shoe industry. As heating systems improved, Mostow has noted, hemlines rose and revealed a woman's footwear; as lighting systems improved, shoes became more visible; as trolleys and automobiles became the preferred modes of travel and as sidewalk and street surfaces were made smoother, whether a shoe lasted a long time became less important. Between 1910 and 1925 the women's shoe industry became fashion-oriented, and the "welts" of the earlier generation were replaced by "novelty" shoes whose styles changed every season. One shoe manufacturer bemoaned how drastically the industry had changed

in a 1923 issue of *American Shoemaker.* "The shoe industry is no longer regulated by the seasons of the year, like the farming industry, but is regulated by the fancies of shoemaking or shoe wearing people," he wrote. ". . .the novelty shoe industry is today more than seasonal. It is capricious." This revolution in the shoe industry favored smaller shops over larger ones, for smaller manufacturers found it easier to retool to accommodate these style changes and seem to have been quicker to recognize that shoe shop owners had to become merchandisers as well as manufacturers.

Other trends in the industry did not bode well for the established shoe shops of Lynn. In the nineteenth century, the high-quality staple shoes made in the city were shipped to rural and small-town markets in the West and South, regions without a shoe manufacturing base. But by the end of the century, industrialization had taken hold near growing cities in these regions, western manufacturers had ready access to cowhides, and mechanization had made Lynn's skilled labor force a less valuable selling point in the marketing of shoes. Lynn shoe shop owners turned their attention to the growing immigrant population in eastern cities, but here low price was the overriding selling point. "We have been chasing too many visions here in Lynn, and hopping over too many real facts," one

Reflecting the change in market from western and southern rural areas to eastern urban ones, the Herrick Shoe Company factory on Sanderson Avenue in East Lynn advertised its shoes at prices lower than the "staple" shoe of Lynn generally commanded in 1910. With A. E. Little, Charles E. Wilson, and the Murray Brothers, Herrick may have been one of a small handful of shoe shops that began to turn to the manufacture of women's novelty shoes before the First World War.

manufacturer warned in the *Lynn Item* in 1915. "We have pictured every woman in the land wearing $5 shoes made in Lynn, and we have forgotten about the woman who must have the $2.50 pair of shoes, or a cheaper pair if she can get them. . . . Our production costs are scaled up to grand opera prices but what our customers want is 'movies' prices. 'Shoes for the Masses' is the slogan that I would set up for Lynn . . . I don't care a hoot for 'Lynn Shoes are Best Made Shoes' or any other nursery rhyme."

The downward pressure on shoe prices forced economies all along the line, and when it cut into workers' wages and the movements begun in the Progressive Era to decrease working hours and inaugurate paid vacations, the city became embroiled in a series of labor disputes that would not be resolved until the enactment of New Deal labor legislation.

The Automobile Age

In 1887, when electric trolley lines began to crisscross Lynn, the city had begun its transformation from a walking to a riding city. The trolley was always a passenger vehicle, however; horse-drawn wagons, drays, carriages, and hacks continued to carry goods around the city for decades afterward. The widespread popularity of the bicycle in the 1890s stimulated a new interest in personal transportation—and in better roads. Many bicycle manufacturers and repairers, as well as others, began to turn their attention to motorized vehicles after the development of successful internal combustion engines and of steam and electric propulsion systems in the years surrounding 1900.

Before 1910, one study has shown, Essex County manufacturers had produced fifty-four motor vehicles, and Lynn inventors had been responsible for many of these. At General Electric, engineer Herman Lemp and company founder Elihu Thomson produced the Wagonette in 1897, and together they developed another thirteen cars. In the same year, MIT graduate Hiram Percy Maxim, an employee of American Projectile Company of Lynn (a subsidiary of Thomson-Houston), built an electrically powered horseless carriage after earlier experiments with motorized tricycles. Maxim built both vehicles for bicycle-turned-car maker Pope Manufacturing Company in Connecticut. Another General Electric engineer, Arthur M.

The Lynn depot of the Boston, Revere Beach, and Lynn Railroad on Market Street still relied upon horse-drawn vehicles to carry passengers and freight around town when this photograph was taken in September 1905. Known for years simply as the Narrow Gauge, the line's trains ran on three-foot tracks between these points from 1875 to 1940; it was one of few successful narrow-gauge railroads in the country. The trip to Boston culminated in a ferry ride across Boston Harbor from East Boston to Rowe's Wharf.

Stanley, built his famed Stanley Steamer in 1906 and is said to have run it along Revere Beach Boulevard at the furious clip of seventy miles per hour. Through at least 1912 Lynners invented other steam-driven cars, a gasoline-powered truck, and the Wiswell motorcycle.

In about 1901 Lynn bicycle manufacturer Charles E. Whitten had begun to add automobiles to his line of vehicles. By 1907, when there were still twenty-one blacksmiths, six horse boarding stables, twelve horse shoers, and dozens of firms in the carriage trades, Whitten was one of nine automobile dealers in the city. Just four years later, the police force began to use "motor bicycles," and by 1914 the fire department began to switch from horse-drawn to motorized vehicles. Slowly, the architecture of the horse-drawn age began to come down. The city and the Brockaway stables were razed for modern buildings in 1913; in 1937, the year that the Eastern Massachusetts Railway system switched from electric trolleys to motorized buses, the city's last two horse car barns were taken down in Wyoma to make way for "a modern gasoline and service station"; and in 1941 the last stable in West Lynn, near the city infirmary, was torn down.

After 1895 General Electric, which pioneered interurban trolley systems, began to experiment with private transportation as well. In 1897 founder Elihu Thomson and engineer Herman Lemp developed the three-horsepower, 75-volt electric Wagonette in West Lynn. Passengers and drivers appear to have been placed back to back in the little vehicle. The company developed many prototype electric vehicles, but none were commercially produced.

Sometime between 1893 and 1902 Lynn bicycle manufacturers Charles E. Whitten and Charles F. Pollard produced the Eagle bicycle and made note of its first shipment with signs on two horse-drawn wagons. The team apparently also sold High Art and Hunter cycles at its showroom at 8 and 10 Andrew, but whether they also manufactured them is not known. Born in Lynn in 1861, Whitten had been in the bicycle business since 1883.

The automobile stimulated numerous changes in the city's appearance. For one thing, the hazard presented by at-grade railroad crossings became more extreme, and by 1909 the Boston and Maine Railroad had begun to remove its street-level tracks and to build elevated crossings all over the city. Streets were improved: by 1918, 30 of the city's 130 miles of roadway had been paved. Finally, the car seemed to force the city to expand horizontally. In 1910 seven of the city's nine automobile dealerships were downtown, but by the early 1930s they began to move to larger lots on the fringes of the city.

Still, horses did not disappear from the landscape. In 1917 there were 963 automobile garages in Lynn, but there were still 1,159 stables, and the city and some businesses continued to use horses into the 1950s. When blacksmith Thomas Griffith applied to a city for a permit to build a new shop, he told the *Item* that he believed the horse was "far from extinct in Lynn" and in fact was "rapidly coming back into his own as a helper to the business man who has small loads of merchandise to move short distances, and pleasure horses are also returning to popularity." But by 1933 there were only forty-seven horses left in the city, and Lynn's short-lived mounted police force had been disbanded seven years earlier. In the 1930s, scrap metal dealer Enzo "Barchy" Denino recalls, the city sanitation, street, and sewer departments sold

their horses to the Brighton livestock auction. Denino himself used horses and even posed for a photograph with his horse Tony in front of one of the city's first parking meters—"the modern equivalent of hitching posts," as the *Item* put it—a year after it was installed in 1948.

By 1901 C. E. Whitten had begun to sell cars as well as bicycles, and his 1902 catalog offered forty-four motor vehicles. By 1903 Whitten had moved his dealership to two floors at 38-40 Central Avenue, where he remained until the late 1960s. Whitten began selling White and Stanley steam cars as well as Ramblers and Waverlys and by 1910 offered Thomas, Hudson, and Chalmers automobiles. He began to carry Buicks among other models in the 1920s and limited his dealership only to Buicks by the 1930s.

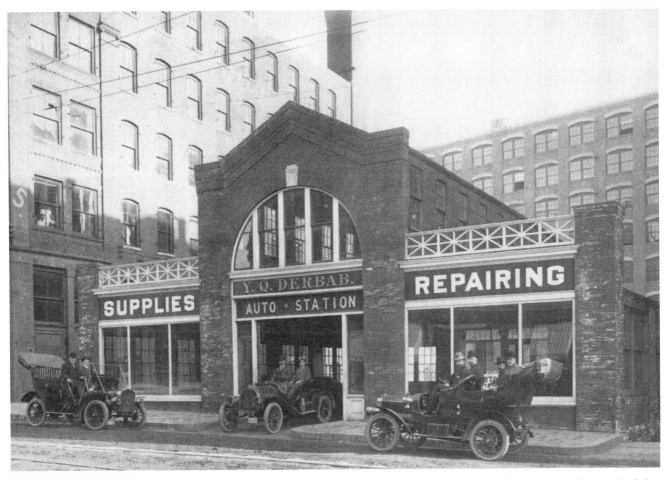

In about 1910 Lebanese immigrant Yusuf Querim Derbab sold both automobiles and airplanes from a dealership at 212 Broad Street; Derbab also had a machine shop on Spring Street.

Ice companies were among the last to give up on horse-drawn transportation. In about 1920, Harry Batchelder and another man posed at the reins of two horses that drew a North Shore Ice Delivery wagon. Purity Ice and Coal Company on Alley Street used horses to carry ice cut on Flax Pond into the late 1950s. Enzo Denino has recalled that the company drove the horses the long way around to keep the horses from having to pull their heavy loads uphill.

Lynn had numerous organized charities to support working people who fell into hard times. The Women's Union for Christian Work, founded in 1869, was one of the oldest charities in the city when it occupied the former Parrott home on Olive Street in East Lynn in about 1910. The union offered sewing and mending bureaus, an "industrial relief laundry," and emergency assistance "all within easy access to the needy." The Lynn Workingmen's Home occupied the former J. Collins house at 13 Commercial Street in 1902. Women's Union photograph courtesy Les Matthews.

By 1915 the urban landscape was one in which cars and horses competed. At the corner of Silsbee and Broad streets, a car flies by horse-drawn wagons parked by the curbs.

By 1907 population was growing so rapidly in Lynn that the city was compelled to erect a series of portable school buildings on Walnut, Childs, and Shepard streets as it prepared to undertake a massive campaign to replace all its old wooden schoolhouses with new brick ones. Between 1900 and the outbreak of the First World War the city built at least five new grammar schools, including Bacheller, Bruce, Chatham Street, Brickett, Washington (above), and Lynn Woods.

In 1912 workers from A. E. Little Shoe Company loaded shoes onto a truck for shipment to England. "Every American citizen naturally feels proud of the wonderful success achieved by Sorosis abroad," one 1902 company pamphlet declared. "Sorosis is a National Institution and in its line it represents the highest development of the skill and ingenuity of our whole country." A. E. Little claimed that the shoe had single-handedly "reversed foreign trade situations. Before its perfection, English and French shoes were largely sold in America. Now the most eagerly sought footwear in the Old-World centers of style and fashion is the Perfected American shoe, made under the trade-mark name of Sorosis."

In the late 1890s the rage of bicycling stimulated a nationwide effort—helped along by farmers interested in better roads to market—to improve the roads, much neglected for most of the nineteenth century when people and goods traveled largely by train. In 1907 Lynn's Clover Cycle Club went on outings like this one, an unidentified bicycle road race and fair.

In 1912 Charles S. Sanborn, a partner in the Lynn dry goods firm Burrows and Sanborn, owned a six-cylinder Packard, among the ten percent of American-made cars that cost more than four thousand dollars. Forty models were made for this high-end consumer, as many as were made for car buyers who could afford to spend twelve hundred dollars or less. Like many early car owners, Sanborn was affluent, and among such consumers the automobile was a recreational toy more than a business necessity.

In 1924 and 1925 Lynn's Leader Oil Company opened two filling stations for automobiles in the city. The first, at 423 Union Street in Central Square, was among nine in the city in 1924; the second (shown here) opened the following year at Essex and Fayette streets. Leader gas was one of a multiplicity of brands available to motorists in the 1920s.

Just as bicyclists had formed cycle clubs at the end of the previous century, motorcyclists were club-oriented in the twentieth. Here, the Bay State MotorCycle Club stopped for the photographer in front of the library in City Hall Square on its way through Lynn in about 1915.

In 1923 Lynn policeman John Hines on his horse Harry L. accompanied the doll parade at Cobbet School. From that year until 1926, Hines (and occasional alternate Pat Cuffe) was the city's only mounted patrolman; Lynn wigmaker Harry Lombard had donated Harry L. to the city for Hines's use. In 1926, when Ralph S. Bauer became mayor, he ordered Hines to motorcycle duty, and Harry L. was given to the army unit stationed at Fort Devens in Ayer.

Before 1908 one of the landmarks of Central Square was Earl's Lunch, long frequented by shoeworkers. The restaurant closed that year when its space was given over to the elevation of Boston and Maine railroad infrastructure.

Lynn's first automatic traffic signal was installed at the busy intersection of Federal Street and Market Square in the 1920s.

On Commercial Street near Hoag and Walden's two shoe factories and the leather remnants firm of Jacob and Jacobson in 1909, the Boston and Maine railroad tracks intersected with the tracks of the Bay State Street Railway until the B&M tracks were elevated. The latter shot was taken when construction was not quite complete. Grade crossings were slowly eliminated all over the city between September 1909 and August 1913. Inbound Boston and Maine service was inaugurated four days earlier; the Central Square station opened February 15, 1914.

The Boston and Maine Railroad ran two steam railway lines through Lynn, the Eastern Division and the Saugus branch. Its large freight yard, shown here in 1912, was on Market Street, a site now occupied by stores, Century Bank, and NYNEX.

On August 17, 1913, the first outbound Boston and Maine train to run over the elevated structure in Central Square drew a large crowd of spectators. While they supported removing the train tracks from grade level, many Lynners had argued against elevating them in favor of running them underground; a bridge, they claimed, would not only be a "monstrosity" but would cut downtown Lynn in two. Boston and Maine planners dismissed the underground plan as too expensive, however, and the rail lines have run on an elevated structure ever since.

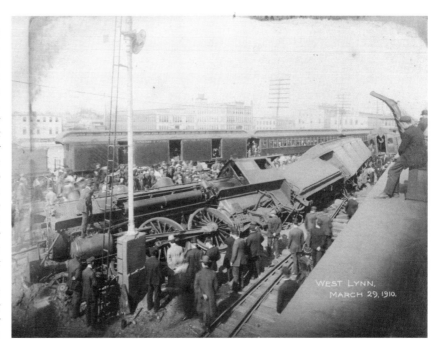

On March 29, 1910, an express Boston and Maine train from Portland jumped the main Eastern Division tracks, ploughed through a ditch of sand separating the main line from the Saugus Branch tracks, and landed on its side near the switch tower at the railroad's West Lynn yards. None of the crew or the train's thirty-five passengers were hurt. "Railroad men who would talk ascribe the wreck to an open switch" between the two tracks, the Lynn Item reported. An American Express messenger in the baggage car claimed his life was saved as he was thrown against Nero, a prize-winning Newfoundland whose Portland mistress was in the car just behind; the dog broke his fall as the car tipped over and kept him from serious injury.

Through much of the nineteenth century, private businesses and individuals owned Lynn's entire shoreline and protected their properties from the ocean with wooden or stone seawalls. But by 1903 both the city and the state had begun to claim and create scenic public lands along the waterfront. The state's Metropolitan Park Commission (subsumed in the new Metropolitan District Commission in 1919), earlier thwarted in its efforts to acquire Lynn Woods for its regionwide system of open space and the city's water supply for the region's use, had begun to purchase Lynn shorefront land and to build new seawalls in preparation for its Lynn/Nahant Beach Reservation and a connecting parkway, Lynn Shore Drive, completed in 1907. Photograph of road under construction courtesy Metropolitan District Commission; completed road photograph courtesy William Conway.

Building the western end of Lynn Shore Drive involved moving houses from Woodbury's Point. In 1907 three houses along the foot of Atlantic Terrace were lifted and floated on barges to Nahant.

Surf Lynn Beach

Recreational uses of Lynn's shoreline became more popular after the Metropolitan Park Commission created
the Lynn/Nahant Beach Reservation, part of its regionwide system of open land. Men photographed and
motorists admired the wild surf at Lynn Beach, and
Lynners could listen to bandstand music, picnic, send
their children to the playground, and rent bathing suits
for "surf bathing" at Lynn Beach (right). The bath
house was built in 1907, the year Lynn Shore Drive
was opened for traffic.

About 1910 the heart-shaped Goldfish Pond in East Lynn was a popular spot. Originally a swamp whose muds were summer beds for livestock
and fertilizer for farmers, Goldfish Pond earned its name from its healthy population of goldfish, stocked by Lynn boys as early as 1837. Each
spring city children fished the pond and sold the fish for fishbowls all over the city. In 1870 the alder bushes on the islet in the center were
chopped down and their roots covered with mud dredged from the swamp; in 1889 the actor Charles E. Davis (also known as Alvin Joslin)
planted the elm that stood on the island for decades. The bandstand at the indenture of the heart replaced an earlier structure in 1897 and
was the site of summer concerts for many years. Photograph courtesy Donald Livermore.

Gold Fish Pond - Lynn, M

In about 1912 Charles Whitten (left) sat at the controls of a biplane with Harry Atwood, an engineer at General Electric's West Lynn Works who made the first trip by air between New York City and St. Louis in 1911. Atwood, who had attended Starling Burgess's flight school in Marblehead, made the 1,265-mile flight in thirty-eight hours and thirty-one minutes. On May 30, 1912, Atwood flew the first air mail in New England (a letter addressed to E. L. Clark of Lynn) from Franklin Field in Cliftondale to Lynn. Lynn was also home to aviator Ruth Law (Oliver), who had worked at Burgess's factory and became the third woman in the United States to receive a pilot's license. Just before World War I, she broke the speed record for a flight between Chicago and Binghamton, New York, having made the trip in slightly more than six hours.

In July 1911 Harry Atwood flew a Burgess-Dunne airplane to the White House, landed on its lawn, and invited President William Howard Taft to take a ride. Taft, it is said, "politely refused." Photograph courtesy Library of Congress.

In 1920 the Lynnway Aerial Transportation Company offered airplane rides to the curious at five dollars a head. Airplanes were still novel enough that motorists crowded the road to watch, and at least one vendor peddled peanuts from the back of a truck. A group of largely out-of-town investors had created the airplane company to offer air and sea plane rides, conduct aerial photography and film work, teach flying, and conduct exhibitions at "beaches, fairs, parks, and other large public gatherings." But its proposed airstrip on the marshy land bordering the Lynnway was never constructed.

49

A crowd assembled for an outing of the Saugus River Yacht Club about 1910. Founded in about 1908, the club met every Friday evening at 95 Dearborn Avenue and existed into the 1990s.

On April 29, 1912, former president Theodore Roosevelt made his second visit to Lynn. Roosevelt's first visit, in 1902 when he was president, was a two-day affair complete with a major address from the steps of City Hall and an overnight stay at the Nahant home of confidant Senator Henry Cabot Lodge. The second was a three-minute stop en route to Beverly, where he hoped to mend a rift with President William Howard Taft; unsuccessful, Roosevelt created the Bull Moose party and ran as its presidential candidate. In 1912 ten thousand Lynners showed up to greet the former president, who lost in the general election to Woodrow Wilson.

President William Howard Taft visited Lynn in 1909 during his usual summer vacation at Beverly. This photograph shows Taft walking into the Unitarian church of the Second Congregational Society at South Common and Church streets.

In May 17, 1916, the three-masted lumber schooner Lucia Porter, *full of New Brunswick spruce laths bound for Vineyard Haven, wrecked off King's Beach in Lynn. Staff from the Nahant Coast Guard station rowed out to rescue the six crew members and the ship's Maltese cat, Pansy, who jumped out of the lifeboat as it made its way to shore. When the crew returned to the wreck to recover the ship's papers the next day, they found the cat, who had returned to be with her three kittens and who once again jumped ship upon rescue. A third attempt to rescue both cat and kittens succeeded. At least two of the kittens found homes, one in Lynn and another, named Lucia Porter, at the Humphrey Street carbarns. Area residents salvaged and sold the laths, and the thirty-five-year-old vessel was repaired within a month at Chelsea.*

General Electric's Thomson Club, made up of company engineers, staged regular entertainments including minstrel shows, a common men's club offering in many northern cities well into the 1950s. This photograph of the cast was taken in 1912.

Boot and shoe dealer Thomas J. Baker wisely offered rubber footwear for sale after a rainstorm on May 13, 1915, dumped more than an inch of rain on the city in fifteen minutes. Temperatures ranged from seventy-seven to forty-four degrees within the course of the day. On Munroe Street, the sudden downpour left water standing almost at floor level. Summer thunderstorms often flooded the Mark Comique, next door to Baker's shop; the floor was pitched so steeply that water flowed down into the pianist's pit in front of the stage. Photograph courtesy Les Matthews.

Founded by a group of citizens interested "in work among boys," the Boys' Club of Lynn has been a haven for working-class children since its founding in 1889. That many new Lynners were poor is clear in the photograph of the group posed in front of the door to the woodworking shop of the club's headquarters at 169 Liberty Street, where it had reopened in 1904 after having closed for lack of funds in 1899.

Chapter 3

Ethnic City

When the first global war in history broke out in Europe in July 1914, Lynners quickly became involved even as the United States tried to maintain its neutrality. That year, the city's shoe shops went to work producing footwear for the Allied troops of France, Russia, and Great Britain, and soon Lynn tanners grew concerned about possible shortages of chemicals and hides, shipped for the most part from overseas. In 1915, the seemingly remote war hit home in a tragic way. On May 7, Johnson Street resident Mrs. Eva French was listed among the 128 American passengers killed when a German submarine torpedoed the British luxury liner *Lusitania* without warning off the coast of Ireland. French was one of 1,153 persons who lost their lives in the incident, while Thomas Snowden, a foreman lodging at the Arnold at 162 Union Street, was among 764 persons saved.

In 1915 as well, General Electric began to work with the Navy on ship propulsion systems. Largely under the supervision of Dr. Sanford A. Moss, who had come to work at General Electric in Lynn in 1903, the company set to work adapting turbine technology for military applications. As a doctoral student at Cornell University, Moss had invented a method of producing energy by burning gas in a pressurized chamber and using it to run a turbine. In effect, turbines convert the thermal energy of gas or steam into drive power by spinning the rows of buckets on the turbine's shaft to run generators, compressors, ship propellers, and industrial machinery. In 1915 General Electric combined a turbine, a generator, and

On April 3, 1917, three days before the nation officially entered World War I, shoe manufacturer Alexander E. Little attracted a crowd as company employees mounted a huge American flag between Blake Street buildings.

53

With their guns, bed rolls, and suitcases at the ready, Company D of the Eighth Regiment, Massachusetts Volunteer Militia, prepared to leave the city for boot camp at Boxford on June 21, 1916. The regiment raised additional companies in Lynn through 1917 and 1918.

a motor into a system that powered the battleship *New Mexico*, the Navy's first all-electric fighting ship.

In 1916 trouble emerged in unexpected places. In April and again in May the Lynn company of the Massachusetts Volunteer Militia (later the National Guard) became part of General John J. Pershing's failed campaign to subdue the forces of Mexican revolutionist Francisco (Pancho) Villa. Villa had raided the town of Columbus, New Mexico, in March in retaliation for President Woodrow Wilson's recognition of political leader Venustiano Carranza, and Pershing's troops were summoned to take Villa "dead or alive."

By 1917 America's entry into the war seemed all but inevitable. Wilson had won reelection with the reminder that "he kept us out of war," but he had begun an intensive effort to prepare for war nonetheless. By February, when the United States severed its diplomatic ties with Germany and the Allied embargo of Axis countries began to be felt, Lynners read the newspaper's prediction that markets would be "potatoless" by the first of April. By March Massachusetts Governor Samuel W. McCall summoned the Ninth Regiment of the Massachusetts Volunteer Militia to guard critical bridges, docks, and industrial plants, including General Electric's two plants in Lynn.

As draftees and enlistees began to leave the city on a regular basis, the children of Whiting grammar school in Lynn knitted sweater vests for departing units and presented them at formal ceremonies at City Hall. This photograph was taken on May 10, 1918. Photograph courtesy Lynn Public Library.

Lynn's Fred Hutchinson kept a scrapbook of informal photographs of himself and his fellow soldiers as they served overseas during the war. A model maker and shoe designer boarding at 26 Washburn Street before he entered the service, Hutchinson took courses in photography and photographic chemistry with the Veterans Bureau after the war. After further study at Wentworth Institute, Massachusetts Institute of Technology, and other institutions, he embarked on a diverse career as a photographer for insurance companies, architectural firms, schools, and other institutions. In 1937 Hutchinson worked in the drafting, photographic, and exhibits division of the federal Bureau for Foreign and Domestic Commerce.

Then tragedy directly struck the city again. On March 29 thirteen Lynn men between the ages of eighteen and twenty-four, nearly all of them from St. Mary's Parish in downtown Lynn, drowned as their twenty-three-foot motorboat, the *Moxie*, went down in high winds off Great Head in Winthrop. The bodies of six of them washed ashore at Great Head on April 6, the day the United States entered World War I. The sad accident greatly lowered the spirits of many Lynners, who like other Americans approached the war with real patriotic energy; now that their nation was involved, Americans would do what they could to make the world "safe for democracy."

The War Effort

Five days before Wilson announced that the United States was at war, members of the Fourth Deck Division of the Naval Brigade left Lynn for service aboard the U.S.S. *Kearsarge* and immediately went about the business of seizing German ships and crews then docked in Boston Harbor. The Navy opened a recruiting station in the city later that month, and the Eighth Regiment of the Massachusetts Volunteer Militia—the same unit of Lynners that had served in the Civil War, the Spanish-American War, and twice in the recent Mexican border conflict—began to seek recruits. An advertisement in the city's newspapers advised young men, "Don't wait to be drafted," and in May the guard again asked men between the ages of eighteen and thirty-five, and those without dependents between thirty-five and forty-five, to "be a real American" and enlist.

EXHIBITION

Air Raid on Lynn

By Aviator

Farnum T. Fish

Thursday Afternoon, June 8

Between 4 and 5 o'clock

Sham Aerial Bomb Attack

Over

Item Building and Central Square

Plan to Go Down Town Shopping
Tomorrow and See This Sensational

Preparedness Demonstration

BRING THE CHILDREN TO SEE
THIS THRILLING SPECTACLE!

The possibility of attack from the air was a new feature of the First World War, and aviator Farnum T. Fish sought to prepare Lynners for one by staging a mock bombing downtown on June 8, 1916. Lynn flyers were active during the war: Harry Atwood became an instructor to military pilots, and Ruth Law (Oliver) helped sell war bonds with movie stars Mary Pickford and Douglas Fairbanks.

In June Lynn high school girls pinned "enrolled for duty" buttons on the jackets of the 9,180 Lynn men between the ages of twenty-one and thirty who had registered under the Selective Service Act. On July 8 the first group of servicemen left the city; in a nearby pool room closet, they had left behind the straw hats they had smashed for a bonfire scheduled to take place the next day (one that never took place). Each soldier received a "comfort kit" containing a pipe, a tobacco pouch, heavy socks, handkerchiefs, washcloths, soap, and a cigarette lighter. Women sewed shirts for them in the gymnasium of the Lynn Home for Young People, and Stitchers' Local 57 set up six motor-driven sewing machines in the recreation room of its union headquarters in the Elks Building on Exchange Street to sew bandages and soldiers' uniforms. Grammar school children knitted sweaters for the troops and presented them as each draft group prepared to leave the city. On August 13, 1917, the Army formed an additional division of New England soldiers and sent them to the front lines in France early in 1918. This Twenty-Sixth Division was nicknamed the Yankee Division, or the YD, and included many well-known Lynn men including future U.S. Congressman William P. Connery, Jr., and future Mayor Harland A. McPhetres.

As soldiers left the city, war workers at General Electric had already begun work on defense contracts. Between April 1917 and the November 1918 armistice the River Works and West Lynn Works made brass shell casings, centrifugal machine guns, vacuum tubes, airplane searchlights, compasses, lighting equipment for boats and aviation fields, geared turbine sets, turbine generators for airplanes, ship propulsion equipment, and torpedo detection equipment. Moss and other General Electric scientists worked with the Submarine Signal Company and Western Electric to create a device that could detect submarines. And Moss also began work on a device that would power airplanes flying at high altitudes. At the Navy's request, Moss began to build a turbine that would be powered from the engine's exhaust gases, but his turbosupercharger would not be ready for in-flight testing until 1920.

Some of General Electric's work on submarine and torpedo detection systems was probably undertaken at East Point in Nahant, where the threat of German submarine attacks had impelled the Navy to install a submarine signal station. A submarine chaser was moored at Tudor wharf, military men were quartered at lookout stations in Little Nahant and on Bailey's Hill, and engineers living at the Schlesinger estate studied the outer harbor. In the interests of coastal defense, the longtime lighthouse keeper at Egg Rock, James Yates, was taken off the little island and replaced with a small squad of sailors. The light on Egg Rock had been lit by hand since 1854, and Yates's removal from his post was the beginning of the end of the island lighthouse.

On May 16, 1919, about six months after the Armistice, the city staged a huge welcome home celebration at City Hall for World War I veterans. Representatives of the armed forces received congratulatory handshakes from Mayor Walter H. Creamer. Nearly 5,500 Lynners served in World War I, and 148 were killed in action. Creamer photograph courtesy Lynn Public Library.

On the Homefront

As early as the winter of 1914 the prices of some commodities were spiraling. Lynn homemakers complained about the high price of eggs and the rising cost of flour, but prices for other staple commodities such as bread, coal, sugar, and clothing remained stable for a time.

By 1917 some shortages had appeared, and that summer Lynn tackled the problem head on by plowing up Lynn Common and planting potatoes on it. The city also installed a twenty-six-by-twelve-foot electric billboard in Breed Square reading, "Food will win the war; don't waste it." By 1918 sugar, white bread, wheat flour, and some meats were in short supply, and the cold winter coupled with wartime fuel supply problems to leave the city almost without coal in January. As a result, the schools did not open after Christmas until January 14 and then had to close again two weeks later. That month nearly every industry except General Electric was forced to close for five days,

and theaters, bars, restaurants, and other such venues were ordered to shut down at 10:00 p.m. each evening.

In November, as more than five hundred Lynn men awaited orders to ship out, Lynn city electrician Frank Moody received a call from a Boston newspaper announcing that the war was over. Moody called Mayor Walter H. Creamer,

Lynn's African American community had diverse roots. After the Civil War, African Americans moved in small numbers from the South and in greater numbers from Nova Scotia. But many families had been in Lynn for generations, including the family of Samuel D. Ruffen. In 1907, a time when most African Americans were not hired for industrial jobs other than foundry work, Sam Ruffen was working in a Lynn shoe shop. The Ruffens lived at the time at 51 River Street near Needham's Landing on the Saugus River.

who ordered the fire alarm to ring a victory signal at about 3:30 in the morning on November 11. According to newspaper reports, a musician in East Lynn by the name of Eben F. Richardson heard the signal, hustled himself out of bed, and ran to the front porch of his Autumn Street home, where he proceeded to play the "Star Spangled Banner" on his cornet. Within hours informal drum corps playing dishpans, tin cans, and anything percussive formed up and paraded throughout the city, and those less organized filled Lynn with what the newspaper described as a "terrific bedlam." People rang whistles, bells, and sirens; garage owners attached batteries to car horns, affixed them to the roof, and let them blow; boys and men attached old bed springs or ash barrels, ubiquitous features on the sidewalks outside Lynn stores, to the back bumpers of their cars and dragged them through the streets. As was Lynn's custom, bonfires were set all over the city to celebrate the Armistice. By noon of November 12 all of the factories in the city had closed, and a quickly organized parade marched through the streets before throngs of people.

An Ethnic City

The Armistice parade seemed to offer Lynn's newest residents a chance to proclaim their sense of loyalty to the country they had adopted. The city's Italian Naturalization Club marched with an effigy of the Kaiser enfolded in the hands of four devils. The Ital-

ian Queen Society also came out in force, as did the city's Franco-American Democratic Club, the Greek Sons and Daughters of St. George, the Lithuanian Naturalization Club, Lynn's many Jewish societies, its Armenian National Union, and even the small Albanian society. All had sent sons to war, and some had lost them: in all, 148 Lynn men died in the First World War. But the city's biggest hero was Sergeant Hercules Korgis, the son of Greek immigrants who had earned the nickname "Lynn's one-man army" for single-handedly capturing 236 German soldiers in Blanc-Mont offensive of October 1918.

Lynn African Americans had organized Bethel African Methodist Episcopal Church in the mid-1850s and by 1909 had built a new brick and shingle church on Mailey (now Shorey) Street, in Ward 4. In the 1920s the Sunshine Circle, the women's group of the church, posed in front of the parsonage. Photograph courtesy Phyllis Dykes-Brown Hector.

In November 1928 Lynn's Franco-American Society was among the groups who marched in the city's annual Armistice Day parade to commemorate the participation of Lynners of French Canadian ancestry in the war effort. Photograph courtesy Lynn Public Library.

By the time of the war, Lynn was a much more ethnically diverse city. In 1912 Cobbet, Blossom Street, and Center Street schools all had "foreign rooms" in which immigrant children were taught English. The photograph above is a 1915–16 class from Cobbet School, in the heavily ethnic Ward 5. According to the names one former student has penned underneath the mug shots of these sixth-graders, below, Irish, French Canadian, Chinese, Italian, and native-born children of English ancestry attended Whiting school in about 1938.

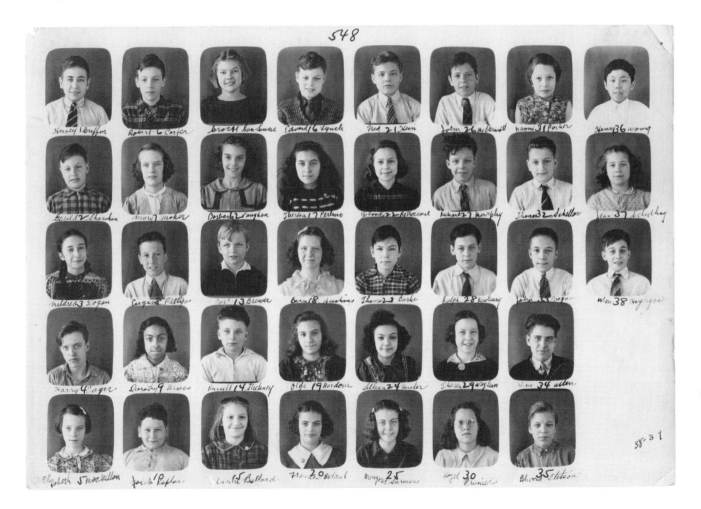

By the time the First World War broke out Lynn had decidedly become a multiethnic city. Between 1885 and 1915 the number of immigrants living in the city rose from 9,800 to 29,500; where one of every five Lynners had been born outside the United States in 1885, one of every three city residents was foreign-born in 1915. And while the foreign-born in nineteenth-century Lynn had been the "old immigrants"—largely from Great Britain, Ireland, and English-speaking Canada—they came in far greater numbers from southern and eastern Europe by 1920. By the end of the war decade, six of every ten Lynners had been born in another country or had been born in this country to foreign-born parents.

Like other shoe centers, Lynn was somewhat less ethnic in 1920 than such textile centers as Lowell, Lawrence, or New Bedford, perhaps because of its historic connections to a vast rural labor pool to the north. Seventy-one percent of Lynn's population was native-born and Caucasian in 1920, a proportion comparable to that which obtained in Haverhill and Brockton; although native-born persons were almost the same proportion of the city's population in 1890, in 1920 the figure included many more children of foreign-born parents than had lived in the city thirty years earlier. The percentage of native-born people in the population of Lowell, by contrast, was 66 percent, in Lawrence 58 percent, and in New Bedford 56 percent.

While not as much an immigrant city as neighboring textile cities tended to be, Lynn was nonetheless far more ethnically diverse than it had been at the close of the nineteenth century. In 1890 about 88 percent of all foreign-born Lynners had been born in Ireland, Great Britain, or English Canada; by 1920 only about 49 percent had been born in these countries. Nearly 32 percent of Lynn's immigrants in the 1920s had been born in southern and eastern Europe and in Russia. The percentage of persons living in Lynn who had been born in eastern Europe alone rose from less than 1 percent in 1900 to more than 10 percent by 1920.

The distribution of European peoples in different Massachusetts towns was striking. For example, many more Swedish and Lithuanian immigrants settled in Brockton than in Lynn; by

In the early 1900s Nora DiVirgilio, Vincenzo DiVirgilio, and Vincenzo's brother Alfredo posed outside their Alley Street home in Lynn's Brickyard neighborhood. DiVirgilio emigrated from Castel DiEri in Italy and ultimately settled in Lynn in 1908. A shoeworker, he lived at 77 Tremont Street before moving to the Brickyard. This view, made into a postcard and sent to cousins in Italy, remained in the Italian part of the family until recently, when it was given to Albert DiVirgilio, former Lynn mayor and son of Vincenzo. Photograph courtesy Albert DiVirgilio.

1920, Swedish-born people were 14 percent of Brockton's population but only 4 percent of Lynn's, and Brockton's population was 10 percent Lithuanian while Lynn's was a little more than 1 percent. On the other hand, a larger proportion of Lynn's population was Greek and Polish. Similarly, there were many more Italians, Germans, French Canadians, and Syrians in Lawrence than in Lynn, while Lawrence had virtually no Swedish-born people and a far smaller proportion of English Canadians.

The French Naturalization and Social Club of Lynn located its headquarters on the second floor of the building occupied by Whyte's Laundry on Mulberry and Union streets in 1912; note its sign on the corner of the building. Groups like this were common among ethnic Lynners in order to help prepare immigrants for citizenship examinations as well as to provide a place for people of the same ethnic background to congregate.

Twenty-six percent of Lynn's population in 1920 had been born in English Canada, while only 4 percent of Lawrence's had been.

Perhaps because the city had been an antislavery center before the Civil War, Lynn had historically also had a larger population of African American people than had other North Shore towns. This tendency prevailed into the next century even as the total numbers of African Americans in the city declined steadily at least through the Second World War. In 1890 African Americans were a little more than 1 percent of Lynn's total population, while they were about 4 percent of Lowell's. One commentator at the turn of the century remarked that Lynn had "no distinct race quarter," but by 1920 70 percent of the African American population of the city lived in the third and sixth wards and by 1940 77 percent resided there. In the late 1920s, Robert Dunning has recalled, no African Americans lived in Wyoma; he recalled only a "few downtown. As far as we kids knew, the blacks lived mostly in a place called Harlem."

Wards 3 and 4, with Wards 5 and 6, were also heavily ethnic in 1920. Fifty-six percent of all foreign-born whites lived in the fifth and sixth wards, while another 31 percent resided in the third

and fourth wards, the latter of which included the Highlands. By contrast, the first and second wards were 83 and 82 percent native-born white respectively. In 1920 70 percent of Lynn's Chinese population, the second largest in Massachusetts in 1910 and third largest by 1920, lived in Ward 4. In 1913, attorney Walter Pyne, who represented many Chinese American residents, suggested that some residents of the city had attempted to force into the zoning laws "class legislation" that would have kept apartment buildings from being built south of Broad Street in Ward 4. The proposed regulation was said to have been proposed to lessen the chance of fire in the ward, but Pyne suggested that it was designed simply to exclude less affluent renters. "The people who have signed that petition have already built a Chinese wall through Lynn," he charged, with no little sarcasm, ". . . and now they wish to build around themselves allowing undesirables like me from the Highlands to peek over occasionally and gaze upon the Lord's anointed." The move failed, and by 1915 apartments were being put up south of the street.

There clearly was some tendency among Americans of the same ethnic background to live together in Lynn. Irish Americans, for example, were more likely than not to live along Alley and

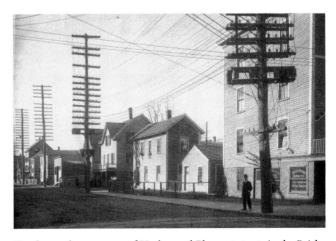

On the northwest corner of Harbor and Pleasant streets in the Brickyard, a basement storefront was occupied in 1910 by a post and telegraph office run by the Italian immigrant firm of Luciano A. and Francesco Cucci. According to his company's display advertisement in the 1910 city directory, Luciano Cucci provided a complete line of services to Italian newcomers: he was also a translator, notary public, customs house and mortgage insurance broker, and railroad and steamship ticket agent.

Sea streets in the neighborhood known as the Brickyard, on lower Beach (now Washington) Street, and, by the turn of the century, in West Lynn and the Highlands. By 1912, the *Item* noted, "a large proportion of the Italian population" was living on Pleasant, Tremont, Blossom, and other streets in the Brickyard; on Edwards and Laconia Court and South Common Street in West Lynn; and on Essex, Chatham, Mt. Pleasant, and other streets in East Lynn. Lithuanians lived around Camden Street, where they opened a clubhouse in 1913. Greeks also lived on Pleasant Street, the site of their first church in 1906, and moved north toward the Common, where their church had moved and their Greek school had opened by 1916. Russian Jews also lived in this area, between Commercial and Blossom streets, along Rockaway and Jefferson streets in East Lynn, along Flint and Wyman streets, and in two other districts bordering the Brickyard and Washington Street. Poles tended to settle in West Lynn in the sixth ward. French Canadians were dispersed throughout the city, although neighborhoods did exist in West Lynn along Morris, Cottage, Linden, and Elizabeth streets; around St. Francis of Assisi church in the Brickyard; and around St. Jean Baptiste church at Franklin and Endicott streets and Western Avenue.

In the foreign-born wards Lynners seemed not to segregate themselves in ethnic enclaves to the degree that existed in the textile towns of Lawrence and Lowell; local Italian-born residents denied the existence of a "little Italy" such as existed in Boston or even in Swampscott in 1912. The mix of heritages in Lynn by the time of the First World War was probably most notable in the Brickyard. Before the turn of the century, the Brickyard was an area about a quarter-mile in area south of the city center, a neighborhood sandwiched between the tracks of the Boston and Maine Railroad on the north and those of the Narrow Gauge, which ran atop the marshes and wharves that separated the city from the ocean, on the south. Initially settled by Irish immigrants after about 1860, by the turn of the century the neighborhood was home to Greek, Russian Jewish, Italian, and Polish immigrants, as well as to people of color who were either African Americans native to the city or emigrants from Nova Scotia and the West Indies. As population grew the neighborhood began to expand north of the Boston and Maine tracks toward the Common. Historian Carl Carlsen has noted that while Alley Street was nearly completely developed by 1905, the area including Summer Circle north of the tracks was still growing; thus Alley Street was largely identified with the "old" immigration, while the area north of the railroad bed came to be associated with Russian and Polish Jews, Greeks, and Italians. As Irish Americans moved to other parts of the city, Italians began to take up the homes and larger lots on Alley Street as well.

The Juvenile Band of Lynn was a largely Italian-American group of young musicians formed by Jerome DelCampo (with mustache and bowler), who posed the band probably on the steps of his Alley Street home. DelCampo's grandson went on to found the DelCampo Music Company of Lynn, located initially at 598 Essex Street and later on Market Street. Photograph courtesy Annina E. McCully.

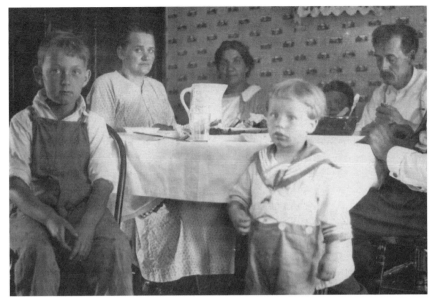

The John Johnson family emigrated to Lynn from Finland in the early years of the twentieth century and lived on Cleveland Terrace in the Highlands. This photograph of the family at dinner, taken in about 1925, shows Alfred Johnson at left, Mrs. Sadie Johnson in the center, her husband John on the right, and their daughter Mary in the foreground. Photograph courtesy Mr. and Mrs. Donald Livermore.

The Brickyard was the neighborhood in which many of the city's best-known politicians grew up, including a remarkable number of mayors. Mayors William P. Connery and his sons William P., Jr., and Lawrence, both congressmen, were Brickyard residents, as was Lynn's first Italian American mayor, Patsy Caggiano. Former mayors Albert Cole, Arthur Frawley, Irving Kane, and Antonio Marino all spent their boyhoods in the Brickyard. So did Thomas W. McGee, longtime Speaker of the Massachusetts House of Representatives, and state senator Walter Boverini. Others who grew up there remember as many as eight separate nationalities living on the same block. Evelyn Lazaris grew up on Summer Circle in a home her family shared with Greek and Russian Jewish families; next door a German family and another Greek family shared a house, and across the street was a family of African descent who had come to Lynn from Canada. Another former resident recalled the business district of the Brickyard:

> On a hot summer's night from Market Street down to Commercial Street I remember the little stores that lined the walk; Italian stores, Jewish stores, Greek stores. Saturday night was the big shopping night then. You could walk down Summer Street; even eight, nine o'clock at night you'd see all the old-timers sitting out on the sidewalk on orange crates and milk crates just gabbing and playing checkers. . . . I think of them days and think, them were nice days.

Presumably photographed while she was on a break, a Mrs. Antolina worked at A. E. Little Shoe Company in about 1910. Lynn employed a higher percentage of married women in its shoe factories than any other city in Massachusetts in 1915; by 1920 30,273 women aged fifteen and older worked in shoe factories across the state.

Other Lynn neighborhoods were ethnically diverse, but probably not to the degree that center-city ones like the Brickyard were. Dunning has stated that English, Irish, French Canadian, Scandinavian, and German families lived in Wyoma, along with far smaller numbers of Italian, Greek, and Armenian families and still fewer numbers of Jewish families. Jerome DelCampo, founder of the Juvenile Band of Lynn, told his family that when he moved from his first Lynn home on Alley Street to Rogers Avenue, at the foot of the largely Irish American Highlands neighborhood, five families moved away because he was Italian.

Of all ethnic Lynners, the Irish were first to arrive, and it is thought that many had first seen

Not all Jewish immigrants went into the shoe industry; in this view, taken in about 1920, Morris Sachar delivered goods to customers for Lynn Baking Company. The overalls and the basket were required of delivery men. Photograph courtesy Bernice Sommerstein.

the town while they worked as laborers on the Eastern (later Boston and Maine) Railroad as it built tracks north from Boston in 1837 and 1838. The emigration of Jewish people from Russia and Poland began very slowly just before the Civil War, and both French and English Canadians began to emigrate after the Civil War. Before the turn of the century, Swedes and other Scandinavians were numerous enough to have formed three churches, and Jewish immigrants had formed the Hebrew Benevolent Society in 1886. By the early 1890s Italian and Greek names began to appear in Lynn directories, and around 1904 Polish Catholics had also begun to settle in the city. By 1907 Greek immigrants had established St. George's Hellenic (Greek Orthodox) Church, Poles had opened St. Michael's Archangel on Cottage and Summer streets, and the city's Jewish population had started a second synagogue. By the time of the First World War, Lynn was home to about two thousand persons each who had emigrated from French Canada, Greece, and Italy, about three thousand Russian Jewish immigrants, probably more than four thousand Irish, and about one thousand persons each from Poland and Sweden.

Many of those who immigrated to Lynn had had shoemaking experience in their native countries, often in villages or small towns where they had made shoes entirely by hand. In the American shoe industry, historian John Cumbler has noted, a little more than 40 percent of the immigrant work force had shoemaking skills. In Lynn, 46 percent of French Canadians, just less than 49 percent of Russian Jews, and 88 percent of Italians had had prior experience in the shoe trades. One historian of the Greek community in Lynn has stated that the first Greek in the city, Anastasios Moshides, was a shoemaker brought to Lynn at the behest of the United Shoe Machinery Corporation in 1892 to learn the trade as Lynn practiced it and teach it to other Greek immigrants. Around the turn of the century, immigrants with few skills were more apt to find jobs in Lynn's tanneries, whose work force was 60 percent foreign-born. One Lynner who worked in a tannery during his schoolboy sum-

In 1929 at the city's tercentenary, forty-nine Greek children marched in native costume in the huge parade marking the anniversary. Here they marched through City Hall Square past the Ravin and Gordon building at 1 Market Street.

mers recalled the ethnic composition of the workers:

> When I was seventeen, I went to work in the tannieres. I think it was on Harbour St. It was hard work. What they did, they had these guys, a lot of them were Polish and Russians. They would take this big hide and they would lay it over a plywood board—4 by 8 foot, tack it using about two inch nails. They'd tack the ends of the hides onto the boards and put them in a place to dry where there was a lot of heat. My job was to take off the nails and then put the hides on a stack. I had to wear a bandaid and cloth around my fingers because, you know, it was hard work.

Within the shoe shops, there may have been some tendency to hire one ethnic group over another. One former shoe worker told historian Keith Melder, "Somebody told me when I came to Lynn. I asked them, 'Can you tell me where I can see a shoe factory?' So he said, 'Oh, I can hear, you are a Swede. There's a Swedish shoe factory over on the corner. Go in there.' I got a job."

The details surrounding the 1910 murder of shoe manufacturer Thomas Landregan and Lynn policeman James Carroll suggest that finding work and living in a new country were not always so easy. Landregan and Carroll were shot on Oxford Street, roughly at the present-day site

Greek immigrants Emanuel and Vasilios Zorzy ran a wholesale and retail fruit business at the corner of North Common and Hanover streets from 1904 to about 1920. The sanitation department's wheeled streetsweeper stands at the curb out front, and the Zorzy brothers installed a weight machine on the sidewalk in front of the store. The second generation of the family, including Angelo and Jeanto, or John, first clerked at the store and opened their own fruit and confectionery shops at other locations in the city by 1920.

Chinese immigrants had been running laundries and restaurants in Lynn since 1876. The laundries were often indicated by a vertical sign attached to the building it occupied, with the word "laundry" spelled out vertically and the proprietor's name in smaller letters above the "L." Occupying the basement of the house on the southeast corner of Liberty and Willow streets from about 1896 to 1930 was the Quong Wah laundry.

of Anthony's Hawthorne restaurant, by three Latvian immigrants who had tried to steal Landregan's payroll. After the shooting, shoe workers in nearby factories rushed to the windows and threw shoe lasts, hammers, iron scraps, and cutters' knives at the bandits, and as they tried to escape one of them, Joe Andboirk, killed himself in a field off Ford Street. Lynn police caught the other two, nineteen-year-old Andy Ibsen and twenty-two-year-old Vassili Ivankowski, and on March 7, 1911, the commonwealth executed both at Charlestown State Prison. "This country of many promises is not quite so wonderful as we

are led to believe," Iwankowski wrote in a farewell note to his mother. "It is not true that money can be picked up in the streets . . . It was hunger that brought me to this trouble." The profusion of lodges and aid societies among immigrants indicates the need to help less fortunate people; according to Nathan Gass of the North Shore Jewish Historical Society, a Co-operative Bakery was established in the Jewish community of Lynn "to make sure there was bread for the workers."

Even though the great majority of immigrants went to work in the shoe factories, there was a decided tendency among some to seek work in the

When they summered at their home in Nahant, the family of U.S. Senator Henry Cabot Lodge often drove into Lynn to shop at the fruit and candy store of Charles T. Venini. This photograph was probably taken between 1894 and 1904 when Venini ran his own business on Broad Street.

Italian immigrant A. A. Poltrino ran a grocery and variety store at 88 Lewis Street in Ward 3. In this view, taken before 1920 and the passage of Prohibition, Poltrino stood at left with Lawrence Pederzani at right.

many kinds of businesses that supported Lynn's major industry. Stephen Mostow noted that 28 percent of one group of Jewish immigrants who had arrived in Boston in 1914 were shoemakers, "nearly five times the normal proportion among Jewish immigrations," but if Jewish immigrants initially worked in Lynn shoe factories they tended not to stay long. In 1915 about 34 percent of the city's employed Jewish population were employed in shoe shops, but fully 50 percent were in trades dependent on the industry; even at the height of Jewish immigration, Mostow found, Jewish workers were less than 10 percent of all shoe workers in Lynn, and the number of Jewish workers in the shoe factories declined steadily to about 14 percent of the working population in the 1940s. And as Yankee ownership of shoe factories declined steadily in the twentieth century, Jewish ownership rose.

In July 1909 one of the fruit stands of Pietro Lucia stood at the corner of State and Market streets. The Lucia family had been in the fruit business in Lynn since 1895; by 1897 Pietro was clerking at his father Antonio's stand at 172 Union Street. Pietro's sons Alphonso and Lodovico clerked for him by 1909, when he operated two fruit stands on Broad Street (at the corners of Green and Newhall streets), a grocery store on Summer Street, and an express service from his Columbia Avenue home. The family fruit business closed in 1995 after a century of operation in Lynn.

The family of shoeworker Joseph Scutiere posed for a formal portrait at their home on Lynnfield Street, probably around 1902.

Many Greek, Italian, and Chinese immigrants set themselves up in businesses to serve the city's large working population. Konstantinos Kaperonis worked first as an itinerant peanut vendor after emigrating from Greece in 1894 and later opened a store at the corner of Andrew Street and Central Avenue. Even as most of the roughly two hundred Greeks living in Lynn by 1901 were working in shoe factories, others had become proprietors of restaurants and *xenodochia*, or coffeehouses, along Central Avenue, Oxford Street, and Pleasant Street. By 1910 Panagiotes Chrisafites, Christos Laganas, John Lampropoulos, James Papadopoulos and Peter Daros, Phillip Petrikas and Louis Praftichis, and Peter Vavoudis had opened restaurants downtown and in the Brickyard. The Agganis family came from Greece first to East Boston, where they sold fruit and vegetables from a cart; like the Maroskos, Zorzy, and Spaneas families, the Agganises built a wholesale fruit and produce business in Lynn.

In 1910 Lynn was home to 113 Chinese immigrants, twice as many as lived in any other Massachusetts industrial city except Boston. Surely, with so many working people lodging and boarding, Chinese immigrants were drawn to the city by the need for inexpensive and quickly produced food and for laundry services. The movement of Chinese people to Lynn appears to have begun just after the Civil War, when one of the city's three laundries was run by the Chinese immigrant Lee Wah at 98 Washington Street. The 1897 city directory documents that twenty-four of the forty-seven laundries in the city were run by Chinese immigrants. The growth in Chinese population tapered off considerably in the next decade, while it nearly tripled in Springfield, but by 1920 Lynn had the third-largest Chinese population in the state. By 1910 at least six Chinese restaurants operated in the city, and thirty-two of the fifty-seven laundries were Chinese.

By 1920 just less than two thousand Italian-born people lived in Lynn, and their numbers remained relatively constant in the city through 1940. Those who did not work at shoe and leather jobs seemed less apt to open restaurants than they were to open fruit and candy stores —although Patsy Caggiano is credited with opening Lynn's first pizza parlor. The Guiseppe Venini family first appeared in Lynn directories in 1888, when Guiseppe was working in a fruit store on Union Street and his son Charles was clerking for him. By 1890 the elder Venini had opened his own fruit and confectionary store at 235 and 138 Union, and from 1894 to at least 1904 Charles T. Venini ran his own fruit and candy business at 145

Broad Street. Unlike many who started in the shoe shops and worked their way out of them, Venini turned to shoemaking as he aged: in 1909 he was listed as working in leather remnants and heeling at 795 Washington Street. Others remained shoeworkers. In 1892 shoemaker Giuseppe Scutiere (sometimes spelled Scudiere) emigrated to Lynn and lived at 2 Alton Court; he had moved to 79 Pleasant Street in the Brickyard by 1898 and moved his family once more in 1902, to 130 Lynnfield Street in Wyoma. Scutiere and two of his sons remained in the shoe factories until about 1915; in that year Joseph began a shoe repair business of his own on Broadway in Wyoma Square.

The second generation, native-born children of foreign-born Lynners, were on the whole less likely to be listed on the payrolls of shoe factories. For one thing, child labor was not as common in the shoe industry as in others, and so children did not grow up knowing the trade. By 1919 in Lynn, only 1.1 percent of all the city's wage earners were younger than sixteen, compared to 2.5 percent in Brockton and 4.8 percent in Lawrence. At the turn of the century in the United States, almost two million of the nation's seventeen million children worked instead of going to school, and in the East they were most apt to find work in textile and glass mills.

In Lynn, the lesser presence of children in factories is attested by their somewhat greater presence in school. In 1920 school attendance in Lynn was higher than in Lawrence and Brockton in all age ranges but particularly notable among fourteen- and fifteen-year-olds. Eighty-three percent of Lynn teenagers were listed in the census as being in school, while only 53 percent of Lawrence and 76 percent of Brockton fourteen- and fifteen-year-olds were. And while only a quarter of Lawrence's sixteen- and seventeen-year-olds were still in school, 43 percent of those in Lynn were.

Children of immigrants were also less likely to go into the shoe industry because, as its fortunes began to recede after 1909, the industry had less need of labor overall. Moreover, General Electric had begun to present a truly viable alternative, and it was nearly as likely to employ women as the shoe shops had been. Lynners may not have noticed the slow demise of the shoe industry as they looked to the future after the First World War; after all, the number of wage earners in the city held relatively steady at about twenty-seven thousand between 1909 and 1919. Instead, what they probably saw was a great deal of available work, in the trades Lynn had long held dear and in the new world of the electrical industry.

Founded by a group of citizens interested "in work among boys," the Boys' Club of Lynn has been a haven for working-class children since its founding in 1889. The Boys' Club provided young Lynn boys with a place to have fun, but, like the settlement houses of the Progressive Era, it also aimed to teach immigrant boys about life in America and to give them skills. Instruction in such trades as wood-working and cement trades indicates that the Boys' Club founders envisioned a life of skilled labor for most of these boys when they became working adults. Newsboy and other clubs were also commonly established to help boys build new communities in their adopted homes.

In 1906 Polish barber-surgeon Joseph Turtowski posed with his patrons at his shop on the corner of River and Canal streets. Turtowski opened the shop shortly after his emigration to Lynn in 1900 and offered both barbering and medical services, such as cupping and the application of leeches; he was also a well-known musician who performed at Polish events throughout the region.

St. Michael's Archangel church sponsored a young ladies' society, shown here in about 1930, which sang Polish music throughout the city. Seated in the first row, left to right, are Lottie (Chojnowski) Twanicka, Stella (Drabczuk) Morris, and Sophie (Krzywicka) Lombara. Kneeling in the second row are Leocadia (Bejtlich) Smith, Sophie (Wyczinska) Dombrowska, Anna (Danisiewica) Gesek, Celia (Wozniak) Szafranska, Julia (Chojnowska) Przybylska, Helen (Zabrowska) Jakizmczyk, Sadie (Karwowska) Kelley, Edna (Drewiczewska) Cowan, Mary (Drabczuk) Kozlowski, Anne Glowacz, and Wanda (Jeromin) Neenan. Standing in the third row are Anna (Wozniak) Estabrook, Helen (Kudla) Young, Helen (Myslinska) Saunders, Alice (Chojnowska) Seeds, Blanche (Sadowska) Efimetz, Sabina (Pietruszskiewicz) Messina, Katherine (Niebrzydowska) Gillis, Mary (Luscinska) Nicholas, Mary (Krzywicka) Dancewicz, Helen (Ziejmis) Dancewicz, Anna (Toczydlowsla) White, Blance (Krawczyk) Alaburda, and Louis (Hanus) Grzybyla. Photograph courtesy Clara (Bejtlich) Zamejtis.

Remarkably considering the circumstances of his death, Louis Kadaveski of Lynn was laid out in an open casket for his funeral in July 1917. Kadaveski, nineteen years old when he came to Lynn from Lithuania in 1912, worked at Benz Kid Company on Market Street. Riding Revere Beach's Derby Racer with his six-year-old cousin one Sunday afternoon, Kadaveski lost his hat and then fell from the car into the path of an uncoming one racing his as he attempted to retrieve it. The car dragged his body thirty-five feet before stopping, and nearly every bone in Kadaveski's body was broken. Kadaveski lived at 8 Aaron Court. Photograph courtesy John Kobuszewski.

In 1921 or 1922 the large family of Rachel and Haskel Garfinkel gathered at the Anshai Sfard temple at the corner of Commercial and South Common streets to celebrate the couple's fiftieth wedding anniversary. The Anshai Sfard congregation was also known as the russische schul, formed in 1898 by Russian Jews from the southern pale of settlement between Odessa and Kiev in Ukraine. In 1919 the congregation purchased the Old Tunnel Meeting House (the Second Universalist Church). A larger group of Russian Jewish immigrants, largely from the northern pale in Lithuania, had formed the congregation Ahabat Shalom, or litvitsche schul, in 1899 and opened the city's first synagogue in 1905. Photograph courtesy North Shore Jewish Historical Society.

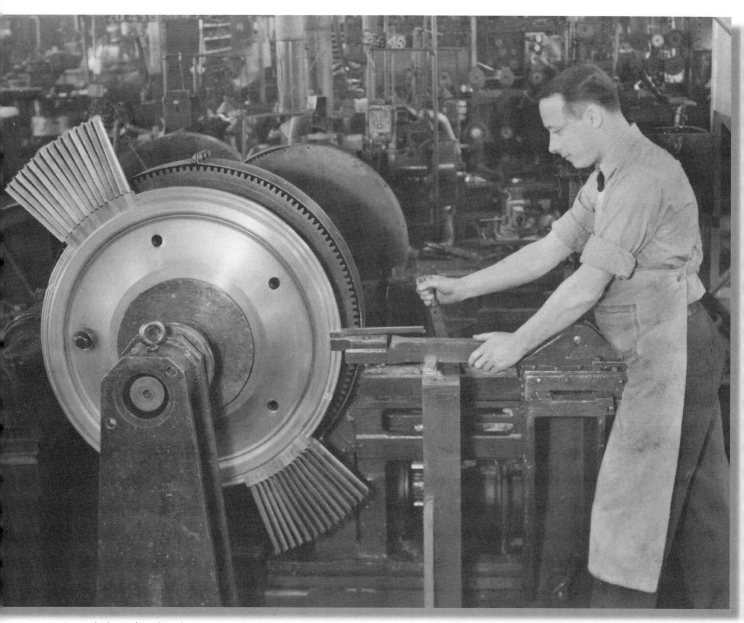

General Electric's turbine business was booming by the 1920s and given a significant boost by military contracts. Above, Thomas M. Carswell, a graduate of the company's apprentice program, assembles turbine bucket wheels and shroud rings at Building 66 of the River Works in the early 1940s.

Chapter 4

Lynn between the Wars

A s the war ended, Lynn was home to about 100,000 people, was the seventh-largest city in Massachusetts, and was still growing. Like other American communities, it suffered the brunt of postwar inflation—in 1918 even the *Item* was forced to raise its newsstand price from a penny, for the first time since it began publishing in 1877—but by 1919 prosperity dulled inflation's edge. Nineteen nineteen was the decade's most prosperous year. Local industry was fully engaged as it turned out some $110 million worth of shoes, shoe products and machinery, and electrical products. That year, Red Sox star Babe Ruth visited the city and hit a home run out of Little River (now Barry) Park in an exhibition game with the local Cornet All-Stars. Over the next two decades, Lynners heard their first radio shows, used their first dial telephones, saw their first native son become governor of Massachusetts, celebrated the community's three hundredth year, and watched as its beloved baseball team, the Lynn Frasers, won the National Sandlot Base Ball championship in 1936.

In 1919 shoes still reigned supreme in Lynn, if not in Massachusetts as a whole. More than thirteen thousand city residents earning an average of a dollar an hour worked in the shoe industry.

Another twelve thousand or more worked for General Electric and other local electrical equipment manufacturers. But the 1920s would be an unsettling decade for the shoe industry on nearly every front, and its star would set almost completely by the time of Pearl Harbor. Even General Electric, whose labor-management situation seemed placid by comparison up until the First World War, would experience its first large-scale labor disputes afterward. Indeed, the most notable fact of life in Lynn between the

This 1923 aerial view of Lynn shows the elevated Boston and Maine tracks and the concentration of industrial buildings downtown. In 1937 the WPA guide to Massachusetts described the shoe factories as "dreary Victorian buildings," but to most Lynn residents they formed the heart of the city.

73

wars was unionization, not only in its major industries but within the work forces of its major newspapers and in many other plants as well.

Much else happened that would make the two decades between the wars challenging ones for Lynners. The city lost four treasured landmarks—the Floating Bridge, Egg Rock Light, the Narrow Gauge, and its intraurban trolley—as well as U.S. Senator Henry Cabot Lodge, General Electric founder Elihu Thomson, and well-loved Congressman William P. Connery, Jr. For the first time in its history, it began steadily to lose population. It experienced two scandalous murders, a sensational theater robbery, and a deadly fire, on average, every 2.8 years through 1940. And Lynners felt the federal government in their lives for perhaps the first time: government action changed the course of labor organization in both of the city's major industries, and it kept Lynners at work after depression struck its heaviest blow ever, here as elsewhere.

Decline in the Shoe Industry

As Lynn entered the 1920s shoe manufacturers, suppliers, and machinery makers occupied virtually all of the city's factory space, and in terms of the products it made and the numbers of people it employed shoemaking was still the city's premier industry. But by 1935 not a single one of the 101 shoe firms doing business in the city at the

Russell P. Gray posed at left in this view of the A. M. Creighton shoe shop on Willow Street in about 1920. Gray was a member of the city's so-called "floating population," having worked in Brockton shoe shops before coming to Lynn.

turn of the century was still alive. Beneath the industry's overall prosperity lay a foundation cracked by inflation, continuing low wages, falling retail prices, competition at home and abroad, and style changes.

Manufacturers and others alleged that both wages and piece rates in Lynn were higher than anywhere else in the country, yet most shoe workers probably could not make ends meet as the twenties began. At a time when the poverty level for a family of four living in Massachusetts was $1,700, the average annual male shoeworker's wage in Lynn rested just beneath that level, at $1,609, largely due to the seasonal character of employment in the industry. Women—fully 39 percent of the local shoe factory workforce—and the relatively few children in the industry probably made half as much. More than half of all Lynn shoeworkers put in forty-eight hours of work a week or more, but many men made as little as ten dollars a week; women and children could bring home as little as four dollars each week. Shoe workers made more in 1920 than they did before the First World War, but the cost of living rose at a slightly faster rate, and the discrepancy between wages and inflation grew more extreme over the course of the decade to come.

Moreover, an industrial depression had hit New England by 1920, and this slump combined with changes in the shoe industry both nationally and locally to make the depression worse in Lynn than it was in most other parts of the region. High wages in Lynn had been based on the level of skill involved in making staple shoes. But as such traditional customers as independent department and shoe stores were replaced by nationwide chains, "house" labels began to supplant company labels. As a result, Mostow has noted, "even the residual respect for shoes marked 'made in Lynn' became meaningless." And as the demand for frequent style changes turned the industry's attention away from durability and toward novelty, skill in manufacture became decidedly less important than skill in design and merchandising. Moreover, shoe prices were dropping. In the 1920s chain stores sold shoes for five to seven dollars a pair, and almost no Lynn shoe factory made shoes that cost less. But by 1933 half of the shoes made in the city were designed to sell at two dollars a pair.

These factors combined to launch a sustained, and, for Lynn, painful search among shoe shop owners for a lower wage than prevailed in the city. At first, unions seemed to have the upper hand as management tested their mettle. Just after the United States entered World War I the city's shoe manufacturers urged workers to join "a single responsible union"—namely, the old AFL-affiliated Boot and Shoe Workers Union, slowly decimated

The conditions of work at Lynn shoe factories allowed workers to talk to each other, which some think fostered the intense union activity that characterized the city. These photographs show the stitching room and the making room of Burdett Shoe Company in 1919; note how the men's shirts, jackets, and hats were hung from ceiling pipes in the making room, supposedly to keep them away from cockroaches.

after the 1903 strike—and announced their refusal to negotiate with the relatively new Allied Shoe Workers and the United Shoe Workers of America, founded in 1909 and in the process of extremely rapid growth. When workers refused, shoe shop owners locked them out. Mediation five months later brought the workers back into the factories with a 10 percent bonus added to wage rates. In 1925 organized labor seemed to score another victory when Wharton Shoe Company, which had contracted with a Boston firm for nonunion strikebreakers, was able to fill only twenty of its two hundred positions and so acceded to union demands. Labor's position also seemed strengthened by the fact that in 1924 a new immigration law had cut the flow of foreign workers to a trickle, thus reducing the availability of people willing to work in open shops for lower rates than union shops could command. A stiff federal tariff in 1922 also seemed to favor domestic shoe production over European manufacture, which relied upon cheaper labor costs.

Yet between 1920 and 1923 strikes were occurring at a rate of one a month; fifty-seven strikes took place in Lynn shoe shops in those years, nine of them general strikes affecting the whole local industry. The number of shoe shops in the city declined, and one local realtor claimed in 1924 that "thousands of feet of vacant floor space" existed in buildings that shoe manufacturers had occupied just four years before. The decline in these years was due principally to the fact that Lynn's older, larger shoe companies either closed up shop or moved to parts of the region where labor was not organized and was therefore less expensive. In 1911 twenty-eight firms made more than two thousand pairs of shoes a day in Lynn. By 1925 only ten of those large companies remained.

Because of the small amount of capital one needed to set up a shoe company, firms could be quickly created and as easily liquidated, and the number of shoe shops lost in the city is somewhat unclear. What is certain is that there were four thousand fewer jobs in Lynn's shoe industry in 1924 than there had been in 1920, and production had dropped by more than forty thousand pairs. The larger companies, accustomed to retooling for style changes only twice a year, were unable to respond to consumer demand for styles that changed almost continually. In 1923 Charles H. Walden announced in the pages of *American Shoemaking* that his family firm, in business in Lynn for 130 years, would close. "We have been for many years manufacturers of women's Goodyear welt shoes, which are now in very light demand, as the dainty McKays are chiefly wanted by women," Walden wrote. "To change over our factory equipment and methods, and to keep pace with the rapid changes in styles and demand for quick deliveries, seemed to us a very great risk that we did not care to assume." Increasingly, older manufacturers turned to less fashion-conscious men's and children's shoe lines, while Jewish-owned firms, as Lynn shoemaker Henry Clayman put it, "took over the women's style business," primarily an urban market. By 1927 one-third of the city's shoe shops were Jewish-owned, but almost all of them were small, and by 1933 fully forty shoe companies in Lynn were making novelty shoes, or "pumps."

Despite its efforts to respond to the style revolution in women's shoes, Lynn's shoe industry was still stymied by the presence of shoes priced at levels lower than it could produce. Even with the 1922 tariff in place, the American market had been flooded with inexpensive shoes made in Czechoslovakia by the manufacturer Thomas Bata, who ironically had learned the novelty shoe business in Lynn in 1920. By about 1923 Bata returned to Europe and began to hire workers whose wages were a fifth of what

On August 21, 1935, the Lynn Item's *political cartoonist championed the efforts of the city's shoe unions to keep inexpensive Czechoslovakian shoes from slipping under the provisions of the 1930 Hawley-Smoot Tariff. Tariffs were designed to support domestic industry, but exemptions for shoes had flooded the American market with cheaper European shoes as early as 1923.*

In 1919 the female employees (and, inexplicably, one man) of Lynn Gas and Electric who had gathered for a Christmas party showed the shoe industry's transition to novelty shoes. The women at right in the front row are wearing the old-fashioned high-buttoned boots, while a few at left have made the switch to "pumps."

Lynn shoe workers could command, and with them he produced millions of shoes that retailed for one dollar, fully $1.50 less than the average retail price of a Lynn-made shoe. (Family member Bohus Bata also ran a shoe factory on Willow Street in Lynn in the mid-1920s.) Imports rose steadily through the 1920s, and by 1929 fully 4.5 million of the 6 million shoes being exported to the United States were Bata shoes. New England shoe manufacturers responded by lobbying Congress to pass the Hawley-Smoot Tariff Act in 1930. The act imposed the highest levies on imported goods in American history, but because shoes and leather goods were put on a "free" list after several years the legislation did little good for Lynn in the end.

The lure of cheaper labor turned the eyes of many older Lynn shoe shop owners toward nonunion areas. Nineteen of twenty-seven shoe firms that moved from Lynn between 1920 and 1924 reopened in Boston or other nearby cities, where labor costs were lower; one disgruntled Lynn manufacturer claimed to be able to make shoes for fifteen to twenty cents less a pair elsewhere in New England because labor was less expensive to procure. Lynn workers willing to work for less could commute to some of these jobs; by 1923, according to an estimate in the *Union Worker*, one to two thousand Lynn workers were commuting daily to Boston shoe shops. Other manufacturers moved north to Haverhill, New Hampshire, and Maine, where labor costs were even lower. Newer firms geared to the novelty market tended to stay in Lynn to be closer to leather markets and the Boston market for finished shoes.

Still, the overall effect of price competition was negative by the end of the decade. Even as demand for women's shoes ran high, and even as eighty-eight companies continued to operate in Lynn by 1929, the number of local shoe factory jobs fell by almost half over 1919 levels, to 6,500 people. The threat of competition made the decade a

In 1922 A. E. Goodwin Shoe of Lynn introduced its Shadow Creation line, shoes that differed from each other chiefly in the size and shape of the heel and toe and in their trimmings—decorative stitching, for example, or the addition of bows and straps. These shoes, sometimes called "flexible McKays" because they were made by the same process as staple shoes except with a lighter sole, were produced by two-thirds of Lynn's shoe shops by 1922. Photograph courtesy Les Matthews.

difficult one for unions despite immigration restrictions. Lynn's Jewish shoe entrepreneurs tended to look askance at the labor movement: a year-long strike broke the union at Jewish-owned Puritan Shoe in 1923-24, and by the end of 1925 more than fifty open or nonunion shops existed in Lynn —including its largest, Lion Shoe, with three hundred employees. The proliferation of open shops helped precipitate the general strike of 1928.

A sign at the rear of the cutting room at Strout-Stritter Shoe Company announced, "dinkers wanted," suggesting that work was available in some skilled trades in the 1930s.

By 1929 Daly's Golden Rule Shoe Company had three factories operating in Lynn. The city's first successful worker-owned company, Golden Rule claimed to guide its worker-management relations according to the Golden Rule. But with the Depression, the company, like others, succumbed to hard times and was out of business by 1933.

The one hopeful sign of the decade was the creation of Daly's Golden Rule Shoe Company in 1924. Company founders called Golden Rule "the birth of a new idea," and it may have been Lynn's first employee-owned shoe company. Golden Rule was formed by workers from Cushing Shoe and was so named because relationships between labor and management were claimed to operate according to the Golden Rule. Former Cushing shoe cutter James "Golden Rule" Daly became the company's manager, workers became shareholders, employees from other bankrupt companies were added to the payroll, and the firm committed itself to the production of "high-grade women's novelty shoes." Golden Rule was instantly profitable. By 1929 the company had three factories and fourteen hundred workers, but by the 1930s it too had come upon hard times.

The Rise of General Electric

By the end of 1920 employment at General Electric finally surpassed employment in all of Lynn's shoe factories. After a wartime peak at fourteen thousand workers, General Electric employment stood at a little less than ten thousand in 1920, and its capital investment exceeded that of all other manufac-

turing concerns in the city combined. The company grew even more rapidly in the 1920s. By 1935 Lynn's two General Electric plants were said to employ more people than any other company in the state.

GE's vigor can be attributed to steady growth in such traditional product lines as street lighting, meters, instruments, and turbines, to its increasing involvement in defense production, and to its relatively newfound interest in the consumer market after 1922. In 1902 the company had pioneered the luminous, or magnetite, arc lamp for street lighting, and many of these lamps continued in use even after the introduction of the Mazda C incandescent lamp in 1914. With the completion of Building 40 at River Works in 1910, General Electric intensified its efforts in outdoor lighting. It made Lynn "the best lighted city in the world," the *Item* declared, so that the city

In 1931 Gerardo Marinucci works on a lasting machine at Gold Seal Shoe Company on the eighth floor of 130 Eastern Avenue. By then Lynn's largest shoe factory, Gold Seal announced five years later that it, unlike many other firms, would remain in Lynn.

might serve as a model for other communities interested in installing street lights. In 1926 General Electric erected "a brand new type of light never installed before anywhere" on both sides of Lynn Common, and its illumination of its own athletic field earned it early contracts for lighting the nation's baseball parks. General Electric also developed traffic signals, including Boston's first at Boylston and Tremont streets in late June 1925. "From the operating booth at the corner of Boylston and Tremont Streets a series of amber, green and red lights can be operated on the different faces of

In 1920 General Electric's River Works sprawled along the shores of the Saugus River.

Just before the First World War, General Electric installed lighting on all of Lynn's major downtown shopping streets, including Market Street, to serve as a demonstration project for other potential municipal clients. Local private business owners also used the company's lamps and standards.

General Electric also pioneered the development of athletic field lighting. In 1927, the first professional baseball game ever played under lights at night took place at the General Electric athletic field on Summer Street. These views show the lighting standards during a football game (the company's Apprentice School had its own football, baseball, and basketball teams) and a night baseball game on July 30, 1928.

The laboratory work of Elihu Thomson, Sanford Moss, and countless other scientists and engineers gave General Electric a foothold in both defense and consumer markets. The bearded Moss and mustached Thomson hosted aviator Charles Lindbergh when he visited the city on September 26, 1930, three years after his historic flight from New York to Paris.

the unit," company newsletter *Lynn Works News* reported on August 21, 1925. "These various lights regulate the direction of traffic, both vehicular and pedestrian. There is also a red unit that is flashed in case of fire." This "traffic control tower" also sported floodlights that illuminated the base of the tower and signs reading "no left turns" and "foot traffic cross on red and yellow lights."

General Electric had begun to develop turbine generators to power trains and oceangoing ves-

sels as early as 1897, and in 1903 the company built another factory at River Works devoted to the manufacture of steam turbine generators. River Works also specialized in the production of gear sets for textile mill loom motors, railroad steam and diesel engines, pumps and compressors for merchant marine and Navy ships and aircraft superchargers, this last product one of the company's most important inventions.

The ultimate success of Sanford Moss's turbosupercharger almost guaranteed the company a steady stream of defense contracts. Before World War I, airplanes had been unable to reach the high altitudes necessary in combat situations because the thin air made engines lose power. In February 1920 an airplane equipped with a GE turbosupercharger reached an altitude of 33,133 feet before its pilot lost consciousness. About a year and a half later, a perfected turbosupercharger enabled another plane to reach 40,800 feet, almost eight miles high and fully a mile and a half higher than the 1920 test.

Under the leadership of Gerard Swope, General Electric also began to exploit the possi-

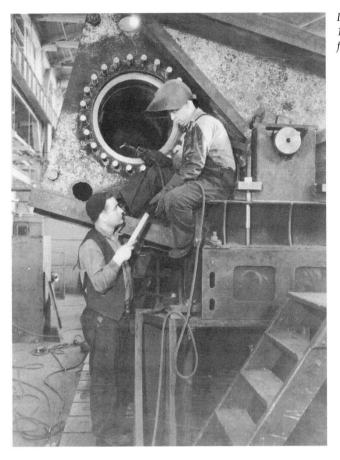

Large turbines, such as this one being assembled at General Electric in the 1940s, took as much as three years to build and were sometimes as long as football fields.

By the time of the Depression, consumer goods had become a major market for General Electric. In the tercentenary parade in 1929, one of the company's floats showed the vast improvement between a colonial kitchen and a modern one filled with GE appliances, and the River Works company store was filled with appliances of all sorts.

bilities of developing electrical appliances for consumers. The company had manufactured fans and lamps for homes from an early date, but after 1922 it began to produce radios, clocks, furnaces, sun lamps, washers, dryers, and, in 1927, hermetically sealed monitor-top refrigerators. By the 1930s, as the durability of household appliances increased and prices fell, General Electric became one of the largest appliance manufacturers in the country; sales of consumer goods helped the company weather the leanest years of the depression decade.

Working at General Electric was a far different experience than working at Lynn's shoe factories, and it was one to which many former shoe workers apparently could not adjust. The legacy of work in preindustrial ten-footers had lived on in some measure in shoe factories, dominated by very small machines which enabled employees to work side by side and to talk to each other as they worked. At noon and after shifts, they poured out of the factories into lunch rooms, bars, lodges, and other places of amusement downtown. Out of these circumstances, many historians believe, grew a relatively strong collective feeling about the rights of labor, which in turn gave rise to union activism. According to John Cumbler, Lynn's repu-

General Electric provided better benefits than any other Lynn industrial concern in the 1920s. It had a voluntary medical and disability insurance program, a fund that lent money for home mortgages, and recreational groups ranging from glee clubs to ball teams. In 1922 West Lynn employees stood by as the company float emphasizing the company's benefits and charitable contributions prepared to leave the company yard; below, employees on break play horseshoes on factory grounds. Float photograph courtesy Lynn Public Library.

tation as "one of the strongest, most militant, and independent union centers in the country existed long before the 1920s."

But many workers at General Electric, like those in textile mills, were separated by huge, loud machines, and much of their working day took place under the relatively watchful eye of management. Some employees ate in the company restaurants and joined many clubs that were also on company grounds. And they were organized by management into an employee representation plan rather than into unions they themselves formed. The pace of work itself was controlled in far greater degree as well. One former shoeworker who moved to GE complained that working at the company was like being "in prison." Like much of twentieth-century industry, organized around a precisely timed assembly line, the processes of work were subjected to scrutiny of efficiency experts after industrial engineer Frederick Winslow Taylor pioneered time and motion studies in a steel mill in the 1880s and had published his *Principles of Scientific Management* in 1911. Yet aside from one unsuccessful strike among Italian workers in 1903, no work stoppages or other labor actions took place at General Electric until the First World War. At that time, encouraged by the National War Labor Board, workers affiliated with several AFL unions and attempted to establish collective bargaining with the company. The company refused. In 1919 GE locked workers out rather than negotiate with the AFL affiliates, and in 1920 workers walked off the job in an unsuccessful protest of GE's proposed use of a stopwatch system. The rest of the decade, a prosperous one for GE, was dominated by the employee representation plan (also known as work councils), which bargained with the company. And in truth, General Electric wages and benefits were far better than what prevailed in the shoe industry, for which the 1920s was unsettling at best.

"In Wyoma as elsewhere in Lynn, the scars of the collapse of the shoe industry were scattered around," Robert Dunning has recalled. "There were widows on welfare and a few unemployables whose plight could be directly linked to 'shoes.' Then in 1929, when conditions seemed to be going well for the bulk of people, the great depression hit with full force. . . . In 1928, my father thought the world was his oyster; in 1930, he felt the world was on his back."

The Depression Decade

The stock market crash of October 1929 ended the general affluence of the 1920s. By 1932, the worst year of the depression that followed, fully six thousand Lynn people had registered for unemployment, and the city had appropriated more than one million dollars for public welfare. Lynn did not find it necessary to set up soup kitchens or bread lines, but in 1932 2,250 families were on public assistance rolls and another 1,000 received soldiers and sailors relief, old age assistance, and private charity. Between 1931 and 1933 the city confiscated almost $750,000 worth of tax-delinquent property. Lucy Nichols, who lived in the Brickyard with her family in 1932, once recalled, "We moved often then because we wouldn't have the money to pay the rent. It was a common practice to move when you didn't. A lot of people didn't even unpack because they knew they'd be there a week and probably have to move again."

"There are undernourished children, bewildered youths running aimlessly from city to city looking for work, men and women in the prime of life broken in spirit and without hope, simply because there are no wage-earning opportunities," said Charles F. Magrane, president of the P. B. Magrane store. Fifty-five families were added to public welfare rolls each week, Magrane added. One 1938 Consumers League of Massachusetts report on sweat shops noted a return to preindustrial practices among Lynn shoe and leather workers during the decades: mothers and children were working nights at home doing piece work, and grammar school teachers began to complain that children were falling asleep in class. As if to underscore the plight of the city, ten thousand people waited on the common on October 31, 1932, for a

visit from New York Governor Franklin Delano Roosevelt, eight days away from being elected the nation's new president. But FDR was two hours late, and by the time he reached Lynn the crowd, drenched by a heavy downpour, had largely given up and gone home.

Despite the fact that women's shoes was one of the least affected industries in the United States during this period, the spiral into which the industry in Lynn had fallen in the 1920s only accelerated during the 1930s. The number of shoe manufacturing companies dropped from between eighty and ninety in 1929 to between thirty and forty in 1940, and by the end of the decade only two thousand Lynners worked in the industry. After a slump from record-high production levels in 1929 the volume of women's shoes produced reached a new peak in 1933, but in Lynn the value of shoes dropped drastically from $28 million in 1929 to less than $5 million by 1940. Lynn's shoe industry had found it difficult to respond to falling prices in the 1920s, but chain stores—the principal consumers of shoes made by many older Lynn firms—cut prices again in 1930. Between 1919 and 1937 wholesale shoe prices declined by 48 percent, which forced shoe manufacturers into a series of actions that exacerbated both the local labor situation and the economic distress of many shoeworkers. According to Stephen Mostow, the average annual wage for a Lynn shoeworker in 1930s was never higher than eight hundred dollars, or about fifteen dollars a week.

As wholesale prices fell in 1930 and 1931 shoe shop owners pressed local unions to accept a wage cut of 20 percent or face the prospect that their companies would set up nonunion shops or quit Lynn altogether. The unions refused, and by April 1934 Mayor J. Fred Manning, generally sympathetic to shoeworkers, claimed in the *Lynn Item* that twenty-six firms had left the city to set up shop elsewhere since 1930, leaving more than 3,300 workers without jobs.

In February 1933 more than 2,500 workers picketed up to forty shoe factories in the city "to curb the alleged 'sweat shop' movement and to effect a higher scale of wages in order to make it possible for hundreds of shoe workers to live without the weekly aid of the welfare dept," according to United

First elected to the United States Congress in 1923, William P. Connery, Jr., was the son of former mayor and Brickyard coal dealer William P. Connery. Called by Roosevelt "an earnest champion of the rights of the under-privileged," Connery was cosponsor of the 1935 Wagner-Connery Act and intervened often in local labor disputes. A former vaudeville star, Connery was popular for his hilarious stories; he is shown here at center telling one to House Democratic whip Pat Boland of Pennsylvania and Congressman Edward A. Kenney of New Jersey.

Shoe Workers business agent William B. Mahan. By March, when more than five thousand workers were out on strike, the state board of arbitration stepped in to adjudicate wage scales, and after the passage of the National Industrial Recovery Act that year Secretary of Labor Frances Perkins ordered eighteen Lynn firms to pay a 20 percent wage increase.

The NIRA only hastened the exodus of Lynn firms to other, smaller places. Soon after Perkins's order, Mayflower, Economy, Barr and Bloomfield, National Shoe and Leather, and A. Jacobs and Sons, all making "low-priced footwear," threatened to leave the city. In October Lowell city employees refused to move machinery from Barr and Bloomfield's Lynn factory in sympathy for the four hundred workers owner Samuel Garfinkle planned to leave behind. Garfinkle told the newspaper that he had signed a contract with the Shoe Workers Protective Union of Haverhill to employ only its workers. As Lynn prepared to sue Lowell firms for offering "illegal inducements" to its shoe firms, the new National Labor Relations Board sent an investigator to the city to sort out the situation. Within weeks, Barr and Bloomfield announced that it would stay in Lynn, but other firms would not be swayed: between August 1933 and December 1934 another twenty-one firms had left the city.

The intense competition among Massachusetts shoe cities for jobs impelled the shoe locals in Lynn, Haverhill, and Salem to vote overwhelmingly to consolidate as the United Shoe and Leather Workers Union in November 1933. But the seeming strength of one big union could not stem the rate war that ensued when the U.S. Supreme Court invalidated the National Industrial Recovery Act in 1935. Immediately, unions in Haverhill, Boston, and Marlboro announced that they had voted themselves wage cuts of up to 13 percent, and Lynn shoe shops seized upon the action to request that Lynn workers accept a 15 percent cut in wages. The unions refused, but as pressure mounted they agreed to a minimum weekly wage of $12.50—below what NRA's shoe code had attempted to institute. Even this did not stem the tide: in May 1936 Dial and Lastwell shoes both left Lynn for Marlboro, and workers anxious to keep Lion Shoe in Lynn formed their own company union in order to accept a 15 percent wage cut.

In the end, what the NIRA could not do for labor the 1935 Wagner-Connery Act did. Sponsored by New York Senator Robert F. Wagner and Lynn Congressman William P. Connery, Jr., the act protected workers' rights to organize and bargain collectively. Connery had also favored a provision that would shorten the work week to thirty hours to "eliminate unemployment in industry by shortening the hours of labor with no decrease in wages." This provision did not survive, but the act did set standards that made it possible for the National Labor Relations Board to dissolve the company union at Lion Shoe. The existence of the NRA shoe codes also helped Lynn attorney Peter J. Walsh secure the agreement of Gold Seal Shoe, Lynn's largest shoe factory, to abide by the code's minimum wage and hour rules in exchange for Saturday work twice a year at the company's peak production times. Gold Seal then cut wages 11 to 15 percent, but 1,200 to 1,400 Lynners kept their shoe jobs.

By 1937 the industry seemed to be crawling out of its worst years. Another merger created the United Shoe Workers of America, affiliated with the new Congress of Industrial Organizations (CIO), and the *Item* reported that 88 percent of shoe operatives, including those at Gold Seal, were "back at the bench or machine with a 15 percent wage advance." The union went to work to try to lure back to Lynn some of its lost shops, but its efforts were fruitless: by 1939 only 1,750 shoeworkers were employed in Lynn, and the union had become virtually moribund.

Meanwhile, worker dissatisfaction had been mounting at General Electric. The economic slump of the early 1930s forced layoffs, shorter work weeks, and occasional weeks off at the company's Lynn plants, and many workers believed the plan of representation was ineffective in protecting workers' interests. "The Plan had no 'say-so,'" one worker complained. "It was just a way of selling Management's decisions to us after the matter was already settled." When pattern maker Alfred Coulthard was laid off indefinitely after a dispute with his foreman about work sharing, he and former Lynn minister Gail Smith began to organize General Electric employees into the Electrical Industry Employees Union in September 1933.

Coulthard and Smith sought recognition from the AFL for the new union but ultimately chose not to affiliate because the federation wished to permit members to separate themselves into craft-oriented locals. General Electric management refused to negotiate with the new union and instead attempted to revive its work councils. Coulthard asked Connery to assist in setting up a certification election for the union and to intervene with General Electric to compel its recognition of whatever union GE employees voted to sustain. Even though the Electrical Industry Employees Union won the March 1934 election by a two-to-one margin, the company stood by its own plan until Connery again intervened; by September General Electric finally agreed to negotiate with the union, and though it was unsuccessful in securing a wage increase until the Second World War the union managed to avert any major work stoppages until after the war was over. By 1937 it had merged with others in the electrical industry to become the United Electrical, Radio, and Machine Workers of America, or UE, and members of Lynn Local 201, including Coulthard, were instrumental in writing the organization's constitution and securing its affiliation with the CIO. Between 1934 and 1944 membership in Local 201 grew from twelve hundred to nearly twenty-six thousand people, even though the union was powerless to stop the layoff of about 30 percent of the hourly work force during the recession from October 1937 to September 1938.

By 1938 the principles of minimum wage and maximum work week that NRA codes had attempted to put in place for American industry became law in the Fair Labor Standards Act, the first permanent nationwide wage legislation ever enacted. With the Wagner-Connery Act, the FLSA was one of the most effective pieces of labor legislation enacted during the 1930s.

Digging out of the Depression
Even before 1933, when the Public Works Administration was created, Lynn had begun to put people to work on public projects that changed the face of the city. The city had built its own stadium in 1928 and the first nine holes of Happy Valley (now Larry Gannon) Municipal Golf Course in 1931. English High School and the Lynnfield Street Fire Station were built with city funds, and construction on Manning Bowl had begun by the time New Deal works agencies began to pour federal money into the city. These funds helped complete Manning Bowl and built the second nine holes and the club-

Between 1935 and 1938 federal New Deal works projects built a clubhouse at Happy Valley golf course, a new stone wall edging Pine Grove Cemetery, and a stone tower in Lynn Woods. Tower photograph courtesy Ernie Fratangelo.

house at the golf course, the stone wall around Pine Grove Cemetery, the stone tower in Lynn Woods, the Lynnfield Street sewer interceptor, and General Edwards Bridge across the Saugus River, named for World War I Yankee Division commander General Clarence R. Edwards and built under the supervision of the Metropolitan District Commission. More than six hundred Lynn women workers were employed in a WPA sewing project, work they apparently preferred to stitching jobs at Gold Seal. A WPA crew also split and cut more than three thousand oak and pine trees felled in Lynn Woods during the unnamed hurricane of 1938. Other federal projects created Lynn's post office mural, and Lynn's Lauretta McCormick Bresnahan became the state selecting agent (and later agent in charge of the New England and Rocky Mountain states) for the Civilian Conservation Corps.

Even if shoe strike violence is factored out of the equation, Lynn had nonetheless suffered more than its share of trouble between the wars. Deadly fires at the Old Women's Home on North Common Street (1920), the Essex Castle Apartments on Ellis Street (1923), Lynn English High School (1924), the Preble Box Toe Company on Brookline Street (1928), and the Hotel Lenox on Exchange Street (1929) had together taken thirty-five lives. The worst was the Preble Box Toe explosion and fire on Brookline Street, which killed twenty-one people—including seven of the eleven members of the Blaney family, trapped inside their house as spreading flames ignited five

nearby homes. Started when alcohol, benzine, and celluloid shavings ignited and set on fire solvent-soaked rolls of cotton, the Preble Box Toe fire was so hideous that Mayor Bauer vowed all factories using explosives "will be chased out of

The 1920s and 1930s saw a raft of devastating fires. On April 21, 1922, fire at the Ryan Ideal Stain and Blacking Company on lower Washington Street destroyed not only the four factory buildings but thirty-eight adjacent houses and the Tibbetts Hotel. Then, almost exactly a year later (April 19, 1923), seven persons died in or after a fire at the Essex Castle apartments at the corner of School and Ellis streets. Though firemen rescued thirty-seven occupants who climbed down ladders or jumped to life nets, some died jumping from the fourth floor of the structure, which had no fire escapes or rope ladders. Firemen were photographed lowering bodies from the windows. After the fire Alice Merriman, who worked at A. M. Creighton and Strout-Stritter shoe factories, was committed to Danvers State Hospital on the grounds that she had started the fire by lighting papers in her room to drive out spirits she claimed were hovering there.

town. . . . even if we have to lose the entire shoe industry in Lynn." In 1933 the city lost patrolman Francis Quinn, shot and killed in a robbery attempt, in 1934 Lynn bill poster C. Fred Sumner died in the robbery of the Paramount Theater, and in 1937 both Elihu Thomson and William P. Connery, Jr., died.

Despite continued high unemployment, by the end of the decade Lynn was probably in slightly better condition than such towns as Haverhill and Lawrence. Even though comparable percentages of its labor force were on government work projects (6.5 percent) and seeking work (12 percent), Lynn was no longer a single-industry town. According to the 1940 census, only 5,275 men and women in Lynn were still working in the shoe and leather industry, while more than double that number worked at General Electric and other electrical industries such as Champion Lamp, a Danvers family-owned firm that had fittingly taken over the A. M. Creighton shoe factory, the last to be built in Lynn, by 1927. General Electric had for the most part stepped into the breach as the shoe industry continued to decline. As war in Europe developed, however, Lynners in both industries looked to it as a certain way out of the economic doldrums of the last two difficult decades.

In February 1933 Lynn patrolman Francis Quinn was shot and killed at the corner of Western Avenue and Washington Street as he tried to intercept three armed men preparing a robbery attempt. Quinn's February 18 funeral was one of the largest the city had seen to that date. His assailants were later captured, convicted of murder, and given life sentences at Charlestown and Bridgewater state prisons.

Women were as much a part of the General Electric and Champion Lamp work forces as they had historically been of the shoe industry's. Assembling household electrical meters and other instruments seemed to be predominantly women's work.

At last manufacturer McNichol and Taylor, workers posed crew on the large model of the company's ski boot around 1930. Downhill skiing had just begun to emerge as a major sport in the nation.

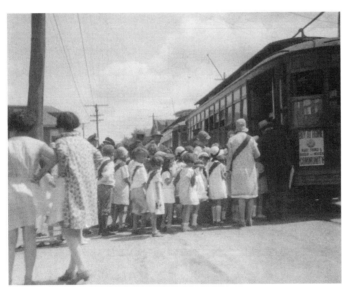

Supporting the homegrown shoe industry was a local effort as well. During the city's 1929 tercentenary, children piled onto a streetcar carrying the slogan, "Buy at Home/Make Yours a Bigger and Better Community."

The end of World War I ushered in wild inflation and then a recession that put some out of work. This wood cutting crew in Lynn Woods in 1918–19 had probably been put to work by the city during this hard time.

Lynn schools were filled with pupils by the 1920s, the last decade in which the city's population was still on the rise. The interior view shows a classroom at Highland or Baltimore school in 1929; in the outdoor photograph, probably taken the same year, Cobbet schoolchildren played hopscotch.

Around 1920 Lynn patrolman Francis Alden Burrill was photographed directing traffic at the corner of Lynnfield Street and Great Woods Road in Wyoma, a neighborhood that bordered Lynn Woods. "In 1928, Wyoma could have been the moon in relation to downtown Lynn, as far as I was concerned," Lynn's Robert Dunning wrote, and his map shows his 1928 childhood world in great detail.

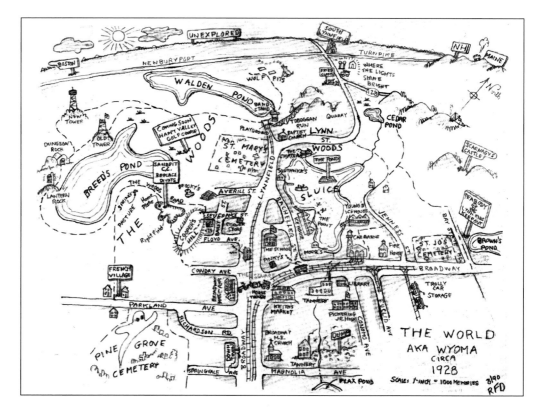

Lynn had been a potato chip center since 1868, when Boyd's Revere Beach Potato Chip factory set up shop. Boyd's is still a going concern in this century, when Sue Boyd posed sitting on top of one of the company's trucks. Another Lynn concern in the same line, though not as long-lived, was Niles Potato Chips and Salted Nuts, whose employees posed by a company car in 1938.

By 1928, when this photograph was taken, Lynn Beach was part of the Metropolitan Park System and managed by the Metropolitan District Commission. Photograph courtesy Lynn Public Library.

Photographed in about 1928, the Flying Yankee Dining Car was a popular spot on Western Avenue that served evening crowds into the early morning hours. At center is owner Jack Hines. Photograph courtesy Dave Waller.

Another popular Lynn pastime of the 1920s and 1930s was the Playograph at Mount Vernon and Exchange streets. By hand, Lynn Item reporters operated the baseball diamond and scoreboard that replayed the World Series before large crowds as telegraph operators received news of the game's progress. Similar to boards used in many other American cities, Lynn's Playograph was operated between 1925 and 1938, when a newspaper strike brought an end to the custom. Judging by the scoreboard, Lynners were watching the second game of the 1925 World Series, played on October 8 between the Pittsburgh Pirates and the Washington Senators in Pittsburgh.

Sports were hugely popular in Lynn between the wars, and the city sent a fair sampling of talent, developed at its high schools by Classical coach Bill Joyce and English coach Tom Whelan, to the major leagues. Shown here, John "Blondy" Ryan (1906–59), a football and baseball star at Lynn Classical High, played in the 1933 and 1937 World Series as a shortstop with the New York Giants. Irving "Bump" Hadley (1904–63), a key football and basketball player at Lynn English High, pitched for the New York Yankees in the 1937, 1938, and 1939 World Series. Cleveland Indians catcher James Edward Hegan (1920–84), who played baseball and basketball at English High, took part in both the 1948 and 1954 World Series.

In the late 1920s the city operated a long, wooden toboggan chute in Lynn Woods playground, a popular haunt of high school students. During the Depression the city ceased to put the chute's trestles in place, and the run was no longer used.

93

Lynners living in the West Lynn neighborhood around River Street Place swam in the Saugus River in the 1920s even though tannery waste emptied into Strawberry Brook and thence into the river in those years. The public beach at Needham's Landing was a popular resort for many of Lynn's Polish American families, and near there many Lynners dug for clams and bobbed for eel and flounder.

On April 9, 1922, the Buchanan Bridge was opened across Glenmere Pond, a body of water that had been crossed by Lynn's famed Floating Bridge for more than a century. By 1918 the 511-foot span was declared unsafe, and a "modern steel structure"—named for Western Avenue's Sergeant Matthew L. Buchanan, the first Lynn man to be killed in France in World War I—was built in its place.

In 1920 forty-three commercial bakeries operated in Lynn, including J. B. Blood's Beehive Bakery and Cushman's. The inside of Cushman's Bakery was photographed in about 1940. By the 1950s most of the city's bakeries were no longer in business, but the Cushman factory was producing four hundred thousand loaves of bread a week. Home delivery persisted at least until the Second World War; from company trucks, delivery men toted trays of breads, cakes, donuts, and hot-cross buns from house to house.

Storm Havoc, Lynn, Mass. Sept 21.38

While Rhode Island and southeastern Massachusetts bore the brunt of the unpredicted September 1938 hurricane, Lynn was largely spared. Trees were uprooted by the thousands in Lynn Woods, Pine Grove Cemetery, and all over town, but no one was killed. Axes and candles disappeared from city hardware stores, and the leaves of Lynn's remaining trees shriveled up from the saltwater spray the hurricane's gales had brought ashore. Photograph courtesy Les Matthews.

The decades between world wars visited a slew of bad weather on Lynn and other New England cities. One storm on February 5–7 in 1920, the worst since 1898, dumped fourteen inches of snow on the city and kept many employees in the factories overnight. This photograph shows Pearl (now Baldwin) Street after the storm had finally passed.

Lynn English High School, then only thirty-seven years old, burned in a devastating fire on March 29, 1924. Lynn fireman Arthur H. Preble was killed as bricks from the burning structure fell upon him.

In January 1937 Lynn's Boston Machine Works caught fire; water from fighting the blaze froze to the building inside and out.

In the early morning of March 18, 1931, the day the first nine holes at Happy Valley golf course opened, the Hotel Lenox on Exchange and Broad streets was gutted by fire; the blaze killed four people. Photograph courtesy William Conway.

Downtown Lynn was ablaze with Christmas lights in December 1953; this view shows Central Square.

A General Electric employee works on a turbine in the early 1990s at the company's River Works.

In August 1979, President Jimmy Carter spoke in Lynn during his ultimately unsuccessful reelection campaign. Introducing Carter at the podium is Massachusetts House Speaker Thomas McGee, a Lynn native; standing just to McGee's right is U.S. Senator Edward M. Kennedy, and to the left of Carter are U.S. Representative Paul Tsongas and S. Craft Scribner, chief of the Lynn Fire Department. Photograph courtesy Representative Thomas McG

In March 1947, a city employee sweeps the streets by hand on Market Street, across from Flaisher's hat store. ▼

Lynn Community Theater director Kevin Buchanan dressed as the pirate Thomas Veal to regale children with the story of local buried treasure for the Lynn Historical Society's 1991 Halloween tour of Dungeon Rock at Lynn Woods. The annual event, cosponsored with the Friends of Lynn Woods, has drawn as many as five hundred participants. ▶

In early May 1993, the children of the Saturday School of St. Michael's Roman Catholic church dressed in Polish costume to celebrate the anniversary of the Polish Constitution. St. Michael's pastor, the Rev. Kazimierz Zastawny, is in the rear at left. Photograph courtesy Lynn Sunday Post. ▶

Sargeant Curt Numberg, a medic at Quang Tri, posed with his public health team while
helping control the spread of plague among the indigenous Bru of Vietnam. Numberg returned
to Lynn and by 1988 was chief of the city's fire department. Photograph courtesy Curt Numberg.

In 1988, Lynn Cub Scouts staged a Gold Rush Ride in Lynn Woods.

Lynn's Sean Holloway served with the 101st Airborne Division of the Military Police in Haiti from September 1994 to January 1995; he was photographed during the occupation of Port-au-Prince.

At 8:00 a.m. on November 28, 1981, the ruins of the Benson Shoe and the Walter Dyer factory smoldered on Washington Street.

In October 1995 Lynn police officer Gary L. Twyman was stabbed to death in a scuffle while trying to protect the lives of Denise Bettinger and her child. The entire Lynn police force as well as Massachusetts State Police and members of police forces throughout the country assembled for Twyman's funeral procession on October 14. Twyman, an African American, was the third Lynn police officer in history to be killed in the line of duty. In these views, Mayor Patrick McManus leads mourners on foot in the funeral cortege, and fellow officers carry Twyman's casket from Zion Baptist Church. Photographs courtesy Richard Jenkins, Lynn Police Department. ▶

▲ *Lynners clamming on Nahant Beach, March 1947.*

Since the 1980s, the Goldfish Pond Association has raised a twelve-foot pumpkin above the stalks of canna lilies on the pond's island every October. Through an annual flea market, the association, founded in 1981, has funded upkeep and improvement of the pond, a beloved spot in East Lynn since the late 1830s. Photograph courtesy Kenneth C. Turino.

After a winter storm in 1946, a Miss O'Neil and Marjorie Tewksbury built a snowman outside the 44 Reed Street home of Ed and Elsie Mosher. Photograph courtesy Marjorie Horgan.

In the 1920s, Lynn Woods superintendent John P. Morrissey created a large rose garden behind his cottage at the Penny Brook entrance to the park. Complete with a gazebo and winding paths lined with rhododendron, the rose garden was a popular spot for wedding photographs into the 1950s. Marjorie Horgan is shown in this view of the garden, recently restored by the Friends of Lynn Woods. Photograph courtesy Marjorie Horgan.

On July 9, 1996, forty Massachusetts Army National Guardsmen of the 101st Field Artillery Regiment participated in a mustering ceremony in front of the Lynn Armory on Lynn Common. Several hundred people turned out for the afternoon ceremony which included a seventeen-gun salute. Photograph courtesy Heather Johnson.

On April 27, 1960, the Lynn Fire Department demonstrated the capabilities of its new Seagrave eighty-five-foot aerial ladder truck at City Hall. Photograph courtesy William Conway.

Frederick Horgan photographed his son Ricky as he learned to ski at Happy Valley golf course in the late 1940s. Photograph courtesy Marjorie Horgan.

When he was eighteen years old in 1969, Curt Numberg enlisted in the U. S. Army's First Cavalry and served as a medic at Quang Tri, four miles south of the Demilitarized Zone in Vietnam. A sergeant, Numberg was photographed that December in his underwear as he wrote home; a picture of his girlfriend and a Christmas candle from home adorned his desk. Photograph courtesy Curt Numberg.

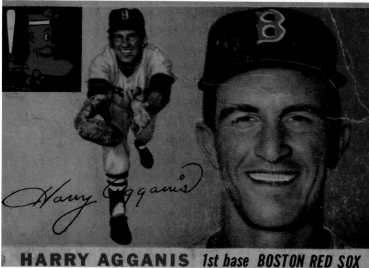

▲ Harry Agganis's Topps baseball card for 1955 noted that after a year in the Red Sox farm system in Louisville, the first baseman came to Boston in 1954 to lead the American League in assists at his position. Born in Lynn in 1930, Agganis was batting above .300 when he died of an embolism early in the 1955 season. Photograph courtesy Robert Keaney.

In 1929, Lynn's Casino dance hall on Summer Street, which had opened as a roller skating rink in 1906, was destroyed by fire. Boston Herald photographer Alton Hall Blackington, who had lived in an apartment in Lynn since 1923, photographed firemen as they tried to put out the blaze. Blackington had been a photographer for the Navy and at the time was a popular storyteller on WBZ radio known as Blackie.

At 6:30 a.m. on November 28, 1981, Benson Shoe and the Walter Dyer factory were photographed from High Rock Tower as they fell in flames in the city's second great fire.

As part of a project titled "How I Picture Lynn," Pickering Junior High School sixth-grader Dah Tach documented the eighth birthday party of his brother Vanara (grinning broadly at the camera with his chin in his hand) at their home at 16 Beaudry Terrace. Eighty-seven Pickering students took the photographs as the culmination of a course on the history of photography, and their views of Lynn were exhibited at Lynn Historical Society.

▲ *Downtown Lynn decorated for Christmas, December 1953; this view shows Market Street.*

For the "How I Picture Lynn" project, Pickering sixth-grader Kenneth Hannaford recorded the demolition of Lynn Hospital, a city institution since 1883. A century later, facing shorter hospital stays and rising outpatient use, the city's two hospitals reorganized as AtlantiCare. Financially hobbled by 1988, AtlantiCare requested and received a complicated aid package from the state, but by 1994 it put Lynn Hospital up for sale. The building was razed in 1996, and a Stop and Shop was to be constructed on its site.

Justin Moy, Chris and Matt Burt, William Copper, Danny Vaney, Joe Illyes, and Tylor Carter take time out from hockey for a snowball fight on January 4, 1994. Photograph courtesy Lynn Sunday Post.

By Easter 1946 Corporal William F. Tewksbury had finished basic training, and before leaving for a year's tour of duty with the Army of Occupation in Japan his family had a back-yard get-together at his Reed Street home. Left to right are Allen W. Tewksbury, Frederick Horgan holding Ricky Horgan, Katherine Tewksbury (later Wrynn), Lorraine Tewksbury, Geneva (Bastarache) Tewksbury, and William Tewksbury, in uniform. Photograph courtesy Marjorie Horgan.

Among Lynn's many postwar projects was a new city hall, shown here under construction in 1949. Many felt the money would have been better spent solving the housing shortage, especially after it became clear that the new municipal building would have no parking lot.

This 1994 aerial view looks east toward the ocean. Lynn Woods can be seen before the water on the horizon and, with Gannon Golf Course, to the right of the St. Joseph's Cemetery, just below Breed's Pond. Sluice Pond is at center, just below Lynnfield Street.

Like many vessels, the City of New York, the flagship of Admiral Richard Byrd's Little America expeditions to Antarctica of 1928–30 and 1933–35, served in other capacities before being retired. On October 19, 1950, the schooner unloaded lumber at Lynn.

Since 1854 a lighthouse (above left) had stood on Egg Rock, a three-acre island off the coast that Nahant had ceded to the federal government in 1855. As coastal defense became a priority in World War I, the lighthouse's keeper was removed, and by 1922 the island's buildings had been sold and the lighthouse beacon (automatic since 1918) shone for the last time. In 1922, as workers tried to move the keeper's house onto a scow, the building could only be moved partway down the rock; when workers returned to try again a month later, the rope holding the old house snapped and sent the structure into the sea (above). By 1927 all remaining structures were dynamited and burned off the island so as to transform it into a bird sanctuary in memory of the late Sen. Henry Cabot Lodge.

On August 11, 1923, Lynners assembled for a memorial service to the late President Warren G. Harding, who died in San Francisco on the way back to Washington after a trip to Alaska; he had served only two years. The service at Meadow Park was the first in Lynn to rely on a loudspeaker system. Photograph courtesy Lynn Public Library.

On August 12, 1925, President Calvin Coolidge made a surprise visit to his summer headquarters at Lynn's Security Trust building. Lynn Police Sergeant James Fee is at left, and the civilians standing with the president are Colonel Edward Starling, in charge of security, and Richard Jervis, head of the Secret Service detail. Coolidge, vacationing that year at White (now Marian) Court in Swampscott while the White House was being renovated, arrived in the area late in June and came to Lynn only three times. His last visit was to attend a flagpole dedication on Lynn Common on August 27. That summer his wife Grace visited the A. E. Little shoe company. Photograph courtesy Lynn Public Library.

From 1875 to 1928 Lynn's much-loved Narrow Gauge (formally the Boston, Revere Beach, and Lynn Railroad) ran steam trains to Boston from its depot at the Revere House on Market Street. The Item observed on the day that "complete electrification" took place, "Something of Lynn died the night the last puffing steam locomotive left the drafty and ugly Market Street station for Boston."

Electric trains ran on the Narrow Gauge until January 29, 1940, when the line was closed down and its cars sold. In November that same year the railroad's Lynn depot, the Revere House, was torn down; having been shorn of its tower in the 1930s, it had most recently housed "transients and families." At the other end of the Narrow Gauge, the ferry Brewster had taken passengers from East Boston across the harbor to Rowe's Wharf. Passengers on the last ride in 1940 took the Brewster's life preservers away with them as mementoes, as well as everything they could remove from the old cars. The end of the Narrow Gauge was a sorry day for many Lynners. Lucy Nichols's mother had taken it into Boston's North End to shop for groceries, but "once the narrow gauge was gone," Nichols recalled, "my mother never went into Boston again."

MOTHER LYNN WELCOMES HER *Champion* CHILDREN

Lynn celebrated its three hundredth year as a community with a huge celebration between June 30 and July 3, 1929. Gwladys, the Marchioness of Townshend and the mayor of the English town of King's Lynn, center, attended the ceremonies with her twelve-year-old son, the Marquis George. Their passage and other expenses were a gift of Lynn Historical Society's Benjamin Johnson and Lynn Mayor Ralph S. Bauer. Also attending was Governor Frank G. Allen, the city's first native son to be chief executive of the state. The city sponsored two huge parades, one largely composed of seven thousand schoolchildren on July 1 and the other a two-hour affair of July 3. The largest parade in the city's history, the July 3 event was filled with floats from city companies including Champion Lamp, top, newly relocated to the city from Danvers. On July 2 Lynn children conducted an historical pageant and athletic demonstration at the city's stadium, bottom, built the year before.

Lynn's current post office was built in 1933; this photograph, taken in July, shows the granite walls going up. The High Rock tower is in the background.

In December 1933, after thirteen years as the law of the land, Prohibition ended. During the dry years, it was said that old fishing schooners turned into rumrunners would line up between Cape Ann and Cape Cod, just outside U.S. waters, as smaller boats transferred illegal liquor ashore; in 1925 Lynn Deputy Police Chief Edward Callahan and Officer Walter Reeves helped reorganize the Swampscott police department after officers were implicated in a rum-running scandal. When Prohibition ended, traffic in Lynn harbor dropped drastically. Photograph courtesy Lynn Daily Evening Item.

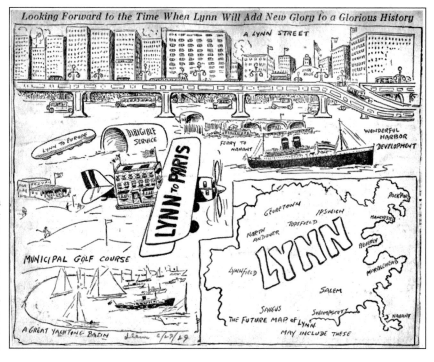

For the tercentenary, the Lynn Item published masses of articles detailing the city's past, but it also called upon cartoonist Jack Beckwith to envision the future. He saw a commercial and a recreational future for the harbor, accepted the existence of the elevated structure downtown but added cars to it, and predicted a wild time for Lynn in the air.

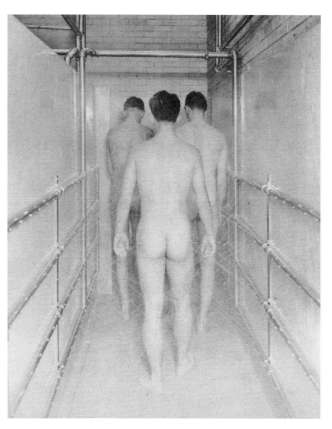

Betty Toczylowski of Houghton Street in Lynn, born a midget, achieved fame in 1939 as one of the cast of Munchkins in the hit film The Wizard of Oz, *one of the first major films produced in color. Toczylowski took the stage name Betty Tanner and danced with her partner Buddy Thomas all over the world—as well as at Lynn's Capitol Theater. Photograph courtesy Anne White.*

In 1931 a new Lynn English High School had been built on a large section of Memorial Park on Goodridge Street. The Lynn architectural firm of Sanborn and Weed designed the new structure and included this view of the boys' shower in its scrapbook on the building.

In June 1937 Congressman Connery died unexpectedly of coronary thrombosis and a gastroenteritic infection, and his funeral on June 21 was the largest in the city's history. The streets were packed with those who came to pay respects to him, and police had to restrain crowds lined outside St. Mary's Church. At the funeral, Connery's brother Lawrence, soon to take his seat in Congress, escorted widow Marie Antoinette Manseau Connery and daughter Marie Therese out of the church; brothers-in-law Joseph M. Kavanaugh and George Rumley followed.

In the 1930s the staff of Anthony's Hawthorne restaurant assembled for a photograph. Anthony Athanas, shown below behind the bar (his sisters Dorothy and Rose stand in front of it), had come to the United States from Albania as a boy and had moved to Lynn and opened his Oxford Street restaurant in 1938. He went on to create a chain that included Hawthorne by the Sea in Swampscott, the General Glover House on the Marblehead-Salem line, Anthony's Cummaquid Inn in Yarmouthport, and Anthony's Pier 4 in Boston. Anthony's Hawthorne was Lynn's most popular restaurant and a favorite among Boston Red Sox players. Bar photograph courtesy Anthony Athanas.

This view of Exchange Street from Mt. Vernon Street, taken in 1934, shows Basil's Restaurant at right and the illuminated sign of Lynn Gas and Electric in the background at left. Basil's, a popular spot, was operated by Basil Hamel between 1932 and 1953.

This aerial view of the waterfront in about 1940 shows the tanks of Lynn Gas and Electric in the foreground. In 1929 the city had built a bulkhead of creosoted pine piles and planking from the Saugus River to the gas and electric plant, thus creating about 155 acres of new harborfront land whose development remained in limbo into the 1960s. The 1930 federal harbor improvement bill and state-run dredging projects in 1917 and 1936 failed to transform Lynn's oceanfront into a major commercial harbor; by then lower rates had made rail transport more viable, and Boston had eclipsed all other ports along the Massachusetts shore.

As the possibility of being drawn into another global war loomed, Lynn was a bustling community tied ever more closely to Boston. In 1940, as the sign notes, thirty-nine trains ran into the capital each day, and the Boston and Maine Railroad had installed two "light writing" clocks, the first of their kind in the nation. Using a "typewriter device" in the ticket office, an employee could post when the next train for Boston would leave Central Square. Photograph courtesy the Boston Herald.

In 1940 Frederick W. Enwright, publisher of Lynn's staunchly Democratic newspaper, the Telegram-News, had lunch with presidential aspirant James A. Farley (seated at center) at Anthony's Hawthorne, across the street from the newspaper. Chairman of the Democratic Committee and Postmaster General, Farley had managed Roosevelt's first two campaigns but opposed his effort to win a third term. Roosevelt nonetheless won the election handily in Lynn, by some six thousand votes over Republican challenger Wendell Willkie, who had visited the city himself in October. Enwright stands at left next to the newspaper's advertising manager, Frederick Gluck.

On January 4, 1945, Boston Machine Works received an Army-Navy E award for outstanding wartime production. Employee Lena Tirabassi, foreman Arthur Courtemanche, Lester Dyer, and general manager Ralph H. Illingworth pose with an unidentified soldier the day the E award was presented.

Chapter 5

World War II Lynn

Less than twenty-five years had passed since World War I when Lynners, like other Americans, were faced with the grim likelihood that the country would be drawn into another global conflict. On September 1, 1939, Germany invaded Poland, Great Britain and France declared war on Germany only days afterward, and people began to worry that the United States would be vulnerable to attack if Canada should become a vast munitions depot for the Allies. Americans were unaware that President Roosevelt had met secretly with Albert Einstein to discuss the possibility of atomic weapons, and the Associated Press released a report declaring that "despite popular talk of death rays and germ bombs" the war

department believed "victims in any new European war probably will die by the same types of weapons used in the last."

By the middle of 1940 Axis aggression had moved federal and state governments into preparedness. On September 16 passage of the Selective Service and Training Act ordered all men between the ages of twenty-one and thirty-five to register in the event "a new citizens army" would be mustered into service. Across the country, local defense councils and draft boards were put in place, and National Guard units were shipped out for basic training. By the end of the year, Roosevelt's Lend-Lease program seemed to promise an active future for industry as well.

In the early years of the war the staff of the Lynn Telegram-News assisted a U.S. Navy drive for recruits. Shown left to right are publisher Frederick W. Enwright, advertising manager Frederick Gluck, and advertising salesman John Galligan.

One month after the Selective Service Act became law, 18,898 men in greater Lynn had registered, including Albert Cole, then the city's mayor. On December 2, 1940, ninety-seven men in the second battalion, thirteenth deck division of the naval reserve marched down Washington Street to the Boston and Maine depot in Central Square, where they boarded trains for Brooklyn Navy Yard. The men had drilled regularly behind the city's old post office at Liberty and Washington Streets before being called to active duty; they initially served together on the vessel *Harry Lee* and then were dispersed throughout the Navy.

Although most of General Electric's defense work was classified, the federal government chose the company's

Soon after Pearl Harbor, General Electric erected a huge billboard with a patriotic appeal for skilled workers.

This view of General Electric's River Works was taken one month before Pearl Harbor. To accommodate its defense contracts, the company built Buildings 66, 66A, 66B, and 66C between October 1941 and April 1942. Building 66 was actually a New Hampshire building that had been torn down and rebuilt in Lynn to store small turbine parts; it was rapidly expanded with wings that dwarfed the original building.

122

River Works as the site of a new gear manufacturing plant to supply parts to the British Navy. On an accelerated construction schedule, the new gear plant was built between August 1941 and June 1942 and designed to produce fifty gear sets for vessels a year. General Electric used three locomotives as stationary boilers to provide heat and power to the plant. In 1941, too, the company had probably already stepped up production of turbines for propulsion and for auxiliary power on Navy ships, while early in October of the same year it secretly received shipment of an engine from Great Britain that would form the basis of a new power plant to propel the nation's first jet airplane.

On the eve of war, tragedy struck in Lynn much as it had when the *Moxie* capsized just before World War I. On July 17, 1941, the mutilated body of 1940 English High graduate Frances Cochran was found in a thicket on the Danvers Road near the Lynn-Swampscott-Salem line. She had been walking home from her job at Dudley Leather when a black car stopped and offered her a ride. She was never seen again, and her murderer was never found. Then, just ten days after

Pearl Harbor, Mr. and Mrs. Joseph Gillis of Rockaway Street learned that their youngest son Walter, stationed at Hickam Field, was missing in action; for some time they and the rest of Lynn believed Walter and his three brothers had been killed during the attack, but in the end the city learned all had survived. Lynn's first casualty of the war was Army Sergeant Leo Gagne, killed at Pearl Harbor.

By the beginning of 1942 Lynners were fully engaged in making the stuff of war. The city's shoe factories were making military footwear, raincoats for the Navy, and other leather goods, and by early 1942 presidential proclamation had declared Lynn the sixteenth most important defense area in the nation due largely to defense work pouring into General Electric. The company now had four plants; in addition to West Lynn, a satellite plant on Allerton Street did "non-secret work," while River Works and the company's factory in Everett were under guard and engaged in work whose nature was known only to the company, the government, and some employees. At River Works employees made gas-powered turbines for aircraft, arc-welding equipment, signaling searchlights, motors and generators, ship

Sanford A. Moss, who retired in 1938 only to be called back during the war, demonstrated his "turbo-supercharger" at a technical meeting. Moss, who began work at GE in 1904, held forty-six patents and died the year after the war ended.

GE was still in full wartime production in 1945 when the company built steel erection facilities 88A and B as wings to Building 88, constructed in 1925 as a pattern storage building at River Works.

In 1943 sixteen-inch guns were taken through Lynn to Nahant, where they were installed in bunkers at the newly completed Fort Ruckman on the former Lodge estate at East Point. Since early in 1942 people all along the East Coast had sighted German submarines, and dimouts were ordered in coastal cities throughout the year. After the November 1942 Japanese air attack on Oregon, defense efforts were stepped up on both coasts. The gun caravan was photographed at the intersection of Washington and Broad streets. Photograph courtesy Nahant Historical Society.

Employees at Lane's Drug Store (formerly Himmel's) on Union Street posed for the photographer in the 1940s. Photograph courtesy Fred Babbitt.

Every mother and father in the Highlands instantly knew whose soldier or sailor son was home by looking out the window. There servicemen gathered in front of Tortolini's variety store at the corner of Acorn and High Rock streets. Pictured here in 1944 are Peter Spheekas, George Patrikas, Varka Kentasian, Gus Belitsos, and Burch Mardigian. Photograph courtesy Peter Belitsos.

propulsion gears, copper oxide and selenium rectifiers, turbines, turbosuperchargers, aircraft instruments, meters and instruments, radio communication equipment, and steel castings. General Electric turbines were used in six of the Navy's ten new battleships, thirty-seven of its forty-three new cruisers, ten of its twenty-seven new aircraft carriers, and two hundred of its 364 new destroyers. Lynn GE workers trained thousands of other employees to make searchlights, radar and radio equipment, and electrically operated gun turrets. The company's most secret work was the development of heavy hydrogen used in atomic bomb development, and two General Electric scientists were among the first to demonstrate that uranium 235 could be the source of a fission reaction.

Lynn was probably ranked so highly among defense areas for its work on the first jet engine. After having received the engine, developed according to the designs of the Royal Air Force's Frank Whittle, about one thousand GE employees began to work on it and successfully tested an engine based on it on April 18, 1942. In June that year the Army Air Corps brought Whittle himself to Lynn, where he assumed a different name and set to work with GE engineers. In an October test at Muroc, California (later Edwards Air Force Base), an airplane equipped with the engine climbed to six thousand feet; tests on a

perfected model enabled planes to reach 47,700 feet in 1943. GE turbosupercharged jet engines were used in many American fighting planes, including the B-17 Flying Fortress and B-24 Liberator. By 1943, Building 29, which housed the secret jet engine development and production, was fully operational and designed to build as many as one hundred of the Whittle-type I-16 engines each month. General Electric in fact built only several hundred during the war, though Building 29 remained the locus of jet development for the next several decades.

At first Lynn's shoe industry hoped military contracts would give it a much-needed lift, but in early February 1943 shoes went on the list of rationed goods. Across the nation the manufacture of women's evening shoes, spiked shoes, and men's patent leather shoes was banned; only "house slippers," infants' soft-soled shoes, and "storm-type rubberwear" were not on the rationed list. Americans were limited to three pairs of shoes a year, to be purchased with a stamp in their ration books, and the style and color of shoes were also restricted. Nearly all of the city's shoe manufacturers promptly received instructions from customers to withhold orders until the details of the rationing order became clearer. Some shops laid off cutters, and the city's fifty-two shoe stores closed down for a day as the

In the last years of the war, the elevated track structure of the Boston and Maine Railroad in Central Square carried patriotic appeals to boost contributions to the Community War Fund campaign. Photograph courtesy Harvey Robinson.

new order took effect. The shoe industry was also severely affected by a shortage of leather; the *Item* noted that most of the city's supply came over "submarine-infested routes from foreign countries," and the armed forces was immediately assigned one-third of the supply of domestic leather.

Because gasoline and tires were also rationed and Americans were discouraged from using their cars, the government encouraged women to stop buying high heels and instead to choose sensible "walking shoes." "Your shoe ration stamp is not a luxury stamp," the Office of Price Administration reminded Americans, but still shoe stores were swamped with customers when the ration books were about to expire in June of that year. "Waiting lines have been frequent, exceeding by far the volume of business in any pre-Easter period," the newspaper reported on June 15. "Harassed and wearied shoe store clerks and managers looked forward hopefully today to the close of business tonight, when the greatest shoe buying rush in the history of Lynn is expected to subside with the expiration of the ration coupon No. 17 period." As the raw material shortage worsened women across the country were reduced to buying shoes made of plastic, and even military contracts could not counterbalance the effect of shoe rationing on local industry.

Industrial employment reached its peak during the war in Lynn. An estimated twenty-

Marjorie Tewksbury (later Horgan) of 38 Reed Street modeled the jumpsuit she wore while working as a precision grinder at General Electric's Allerton Street plant during the war. Though she also wore a headband, she took it off for the photograph, taken by her boyfriend. Photograph courtesy Marjorie Horgan.

With so many war workers in the city carrying money they could spend on little else, Lynn bars and restaurants did a booming business. Larry Meaney and Francis (Mickey) Dolan tended bar at O'Connor's Restaurant on Lewis Street.

three to twenty-five thousand people worked at GE alone, and such industries as Boston Machine Works were also full of employees working on defense contracts. And factories were full of women; in early 1943 Hoague-Sprague Corporation even advertised for "several tall girls to learn automatic machine operation." Elsewhere, women in industrial work was a real novelty, a hard pill for many factory owners and women themselves to swallow; government funds to create day care centers for children so that married women would enter the factories often failed to accomplish their purpose. But in Lynn women had been part of the factory work force for many generations; the war simply shifted the ratio

Opened for business in 1928, the Capitol Diner in the 1940s looked very much as it does today.

of women to men upward. By the end of 1942 an estimated half of the work force at General Electric's West Lynn Works were women.

Lynn's population probably reached a temporary high during the war as workers in search of defense jobs inundated the city. Because it was already well connected by public transportation to other parts of the greater Boston area, not as many persons probably moved to Lynn as worked in the city's factories; still, the newspaper's classified section regularly carried the banner headline "War Workers Want Rooms." By February 1945 the Eastern Massachusetts Street Railway Company put up a bus shelter in Market Square to accommodate war workers, and by all accounts the city was a lively place. Lou Ames, a musician born in Lynn in 1913, recalls that the Lucerne in Central Square was the hottest spot in the city. Arthur Breedy, an African American musician born in Lynn in 1917, recalls having sung in bars and restaurants "all up and down the Barbary coast," an area populated by about twenty bars, including the Dutchman, the Twentieth Century, and Blanchard's, that extended from Olympia Square to Summer Street. As early as the First World War, the Barbary Coast had given birth to

the expression, "Lynn, Lynn, the City of Sin," still a memorable one among longtime city residents.

In addition to the casualties of war—344 Lynn men and one woman (Mary E. Dibble of the Women's Auxiliary Army Corps) were killed in action—the city suffered other calamities. Two days before the end of 1941 St. Mary's Church in City Hall Square, which had served Lynn's Catholic population since 1861, was destroyed by fire. Less than a month later, fourteen people were killed as they jumped from the windows of the burning Melvin Hall Apartments on Spring Street. Many of them died not from the fire itself but from hitting the edges of the life nets firemen held out below, or from missing them altogether. In November 1942 thirteen residents of Lynn and the surrounding area were among the 492 persons who died trying to escape the Cocoanut Grove nightclub fire in Boston.

With the announcement of victory in Europe in early May 1945, Lynners hung Hitler in effigy on Blanchard and Franklin streets. "My memory of VE Day was being with friends from my neighborhood, Collins Street in East Lynn," Florence Fitzgerald of West Lynn recently recalled. "Every day we would get together and talk about

Union Street looking east toward Ireson (now Joyce) Street in 1945, as the war drew to a close.

On January 20, 1942, the Melvin Hall apartments on Spring Street caught fire and killed fifteen residents, some of whom lost their lives as they jumped for, and missed, life nets held out below.

the war. Everyone had someone dear to them serving our country. When we heard the news over the radio about VE Day, I don't know why, but we all headed for Central Square in Lynn. I'll never forget how hundreds of other people had the same idea." But for the most part celebrating was held off as Allied troops continued the war in the Pacific. When VJ Day arrived in mid-August, ten thousand people assembled spontaneously in Central Square and joined tin pan bands and conga and snake dance lines that wound themselves through the city; the *Item* on August 15 called it "Lynn's wildest night." The crowds in Central Square the night before were so large that buses could not operate, the city's largest restaurant ran out of food at 10:15 and had to close, and hundreds of happy people watched a dice game in the middle of Union Street.

Immediately afterward the city turned its attention to the veterans and most particularly to their need of housing. For decades, Lynn's former single-family houses had been broken up into multi-family ones; with the influx of war workers, many of them still employed during 1946 and

1947, the city found itself desperately short of available housing. After the war, Navy Lieutenant Robert Breed walked the whole area with his wife and three children to discover only that "everything was full." On Pudding Hill, Mildred Anderson was sitting on her doorstep when the Breeds visited that section of town. When Breed asked if she knew of any rooms, Anderson told him that her sister was moving out of her basement apartment in a building on Chancery Court. "That's how I got it," Breed recalled.

Solving the housing problem was vastly complicated by the fact that building materials remained scarce through much of 1946, and costs were spiraling. The cost of labor, too, was rising, and when wartime controls on wages and prices were lifted in 1946 rents also escalated. Mayor Cole,

Stuart Tarr and his wife probably posed for this picture around the time he became mayor in 1948. Albert Cole, serving as mayor when he entered the service in April 1942, was reelected in 1946 while still in the Pacific. Tarr guided the city through its housing crisis and its first public housing projects.

back from the war, set the city's housing committee to the task of building "semi-permanent" houses for those veterans who could find no housing nor afford to rent, and in September 1946 the city opened the fifty-year-old Bruce School, abandoned four years earlier as a school building, to house eighteen families with more than seventy children. Then Cole and the city council voted to sell veterans a lot and a foundation on the former city infirmary property on Tower Hill for ten dollars, and within a few years a suburban-style housing project called Veterans Village arose on the land. Two public housing projects—Lynn's first—were also built. By August 1946 the city bought the Chestnut Street land once occupied by the Good-Will Soap Works, housed veterans and their families in converted barracks, and began to build what became Memorial Park. In early 1950 it agreed (in a six-to-five vote) to accept federal housing funds to build what became known as America Park on Winnepurkit Avenue.

On January 21, 1946, six days after the strike began, Lynn Local 201 members traveled to Lowell to picket the General Electric plant there; in the end, workers in seventy-five GE plants joined the strike, one of the biggest labor actions of the postwar period. Photograph courtesy the Boston Public Library, Print Department.

In the middle of June in 1946 war-induced scarcities persisted in Lynn as elsewhere. Flour was scarce, and 18 percent of the city's restaurants reported having no sugar at all. The next month, when all federal price controls were lifted, meat once again appeared in Lynn stores, but prices seemed astronomical compared to what they had been in 1941. The soaring prices induced the most massive wave of strikes in the nation's history, and Lynn's largest began on January 11, 1946, at General Electric. GE workers in the city voted 12,391 to 1,860 to strike on the grounds that the 10 percent wage increase the company had offered was not enough to meet costs in the inflationary postwar era. Four days later sixteen thousand workers in seventy-five of the company's plants were on strike.

During the war, there had been only a handful of work stoppages at General Electric, and the company had agreed in June 1943 to the union's demand that it become a union shop with a compulsory deduction from each worker's wages for union dues. During 1943 anywhere from four to nine hundred employees joined the union each month, and by 1944 Local 201 had twenty-six thousand members. But the need for all-out production during the war had brought an end to many benefits, such as higher wage rates for the night shift, that the union had earlier fought hard to earn; these losses, coupled with wage increases that seemed to lag further and further behind the cost of living, inspired the 1946 strike. The walkout lasted about two months and ended with a wage increase of 18.5 cents an hour. It was only the first of a rash of strikes at General Electric in the postwar period. It was almost as if the spirit of organized labor had left the wasting body of the shoe industry and infused itself into Lynn's new leading employer. And in February 1946 one event seemed to symbolize the transition: fire broke out on Andrew Street and destroyed Lasters Hall, for more than five decades the headquarters of those in Lynn who had practiced one of the most respected of shoe crafts.

LYNN · VETERAN · HOUSING

LOOKING · SOUTH · from · MEMORIAL · PARK

MELVIN · E · COOMBS · · · ARCHITECT

In 1947 Lynn architect Melvin E. Coombs designed Lynn's first public housing for veterans Memorial Park (above) on the land earlier occupied by George E. Marsh's soap factory. In 1950, ten months after the city council only narrowly approved the project, the state housing board's architect prepared a plan for what would become America Park (below), a low-rent group of sixty-eight buildings on Winnepurkit Avenue that was one of the largest veterans' housing projects outside of Boston. As planned, America Park was to house 408 families by July 1951. America Park view courtesy the Boston Herald.

Grace Munroe, a bookkeeper who lived on West Baltimore Street, was the first Lynn woman to enlist in the Women's Auxiliary Army Corps.

Fred Babbitt photographed this Lynn sailor on Union Street with two women who worked in the cosmetics department at Lane's Drug Store. Photograph courtesy Fred Babbitt.

Early members of the African American Barton/Scott Post of the Veterans of Foreign Wars posed in Central Square in about 1944. Crouching in front are Frederick Bradley and Walter Barton; in the second row from left are Aubrey Hector, Roy Tyler, and Joseph Hezekiah. In the rear are John Franklin, Benjamin Franklin, Benjamin Bowzer, and Walter Fowler. The post was named for Charles Barton and Horatio Scott, the first African American Lynners to die in World War II. Photograph courtesy M. Bradley.

Civilian air raid wardens were
recruited soon after Pearl Harbor
was attacked in December 1941.
This group was photographed at
Goldfish Pond in the middle of 1943,
the worst year of the war.

At one of the city's wartime parades,
General Electric workers marched
past the corner of Market and
Munroe streets with the proclamation,
"Producing for Victory."

In June 1944 Second Lieutenant Donald
Livermore of Lynn posed with the rest of
the crew training for combat on a B26
Martin Marauder at Lake Charles Air
Force Base in Louisiana. Livermore, third
from left, was the bombardier. Photograph
courtesy Donald Livermore.

Swampscott High School graduates H. Allen Durkee and Fred L. Mower had begun making what was originally called "Toot Sweet Marshmallow Fluff" at night with a formula a Boston man had developed before World War I. The two began selling it door to door in about 1920 and soon incorporated as Durkee-Mower, Inc. This factory view was taken in the sugar-short 1940s, when the product was made in much smaller quantities, but the new families of the postwar world assured it a healthy future thereafter. Photograph courtesy Durkee-Mower, Inc.

Beginning in 1930 and throughout the war Marshmallow Fluff manufacturer Durkee-Mower, Inc., hosted a fifteen-minute radio program every Sunday evening just before Jack Benny on the Boston area's Yankee Network. The show featured the Flufferettes—sisters Rita, Mary, and Rosemary Gallagher, xylophonist Salvy Cavvichio, announcers Vin Maloney and Eleanor Gay, pianist Milton Brody, and guitarist Perry Lipson. According to a January 1938 advertisement in New England Grocery and Market Magazine, the group supplied "the musical meringue of radio with melody that's sweeter than sweet." Photograph courtesy Durkee-Mower, Inc.

At the Fox Hill Bridge, an enthusiastic crowd welcomed back to Lynn Staff Sergeant Edward "Nipper" Clancy. From a West Lynn family active in sports and local politics, Clancy flew the maximum fifty missions as a tailgunner on a B17, most of them dangerous expeditions over the Ploesti oil fields. Bill McGinn of the Cuffe-McGinn Funeral Home, drove Clancy's car in the homecoming celebration; Bill Toomey accompanied the car on motorcycle. In the back seat with Clancy is his father, John; directly in back of John Clancy is Bill Grady (in suspenders), equipment manager at Classical High School; just to the right of him stands Thomas O'Connor (wearing a hat), athletic director at Lynn Technical High School. Clancy's brother John F. "Hap" Clancy, who became a city councilor and later a state representative, is standing just behind McGinn. Red Burns, head custodian of the city schools, is the first man standing outside the car on the left; Joe Walsh, who like Hap Clancy became both a city councilor and a state representative, is the fourth man from the left, and the vaudevillian Guffer Murphy is eighth from left.

Turning from Oakville Street onto Summer Street, George Alexander drives a tractor and trailer with a separate dolly for the sixteen-inch gun tube, center, en route to Fort Ruckman on Nahant in 1943. Photograph courtesy Nahant Historical Society.

Lynn's theaters, shown here in about 1945, were as busy as its restaurants and bars during the war. Especially popular among night-shift workers, several local theaters added morning shows for them when they got off work. The Paramount on Union Street (top) could seat more than 2,500 people. The center photo shows its lobby. The Uptown on Western Avenue is shown at bottom. The projectionist was said to have had to climb a ladder and go through the second story window (next to the billboard on side of the building) to gain entry to the projection room. Photographs courtesy John Kobuszewski.

During the war, the Dykes, Brown, and Flamer families assembled for the sweet sixteenth birthday party of Ruth Althea Brown at Townsend Hall on Union Street. Shown are Ruth Althea Brown (later Flamer), her mother Ruth Brown, and Phyllis Brown Dykes-Hector. Photograph courtesy Phyllis Brown Dykes-Hector.

136

In 1951 the War Parents and Gold Star Mothers (those who had lost children during the fighting in World War II) gathered for a luncheon at Lynn's Hotel Edison. On June 12, 1946, the sisters and mothers of Lynners killed in action during the war were given red roses at a ceremony at Lynn English High School.

During the war the Tavern Players of Lynn took its Gay Nineties show on tour around the region to entertain fraternal groups engaged in war fund drives. Founded in 1933 in the midst of the Depression, the Tavern Players provided inexpensive live theater for Lynners until 1968; its wartime activity was patterned after the USO (United Service Organization) entertainments so popular with soldiers stateside and overseas. One early Tavern Player, Estelle Parsons, later won an Oscar for the movie Bonnie and Clyde and several Tony awards for outstanding performances on Broadway.

In 1946, downtown Lynn was still filled with war-induced activity. This view shows Union Street looking toward Central Square from Silsbee Street; buses had begun to replace trolleys in downtown Lynn in 1933.

Chapter 6

Portrait of a City:
Lynn in the Postwar World

*L*ynn emerged from World War II with its highest population ever and a robust economy. Fully 125,000 people were living in the city in 1947, and General Electric was then the leading manufacturer of most types of electrical equipment in the nation. Layoffs that had severely affected other defense plants right after the war had only slightly affected GE. And Local 201, coming off its successful strike in the early part of 1946, had nineteen thousand members, which made it the largest union in Lynn, the largest local in the United Electrical union, and one of the largest locals in the commonwealth. By 1949 the city produced more than 185 million dollars worth of goods in 369 manufacturing plants. Seven of them produced electrical goods, while eighty-four firms were in business making boots and shoes and cut stocks and findings. Four tanneries were still operating in Lynn, as was Lydia Pinkham's seventy-year-old medicine business, which employed 170 in the factory and 200 salespeople on the road.

Lynn was in the midst of trying to solve its housing shortage in 1947 when it embarked

As veterans were still returning from the Second World War, young Lynn men were being recruited for a standing army as Americans confronted an age of perpetual preparedness. These young men, dining at Basil's Restaurant in Lynn with the city's war hero, Sergeant Sam Moody (seated at rear right), had just signed up to serve.

In 1947 movie star Martha Raye came to Lynn to boost recruiting efforts. Standing at Raye's left is Lynn native Sam Moody, who had survived the Bataan Death March and had been a prisoner of war from April 1942 to September 1946. At the end of the year Moody flew to Asia to testify against alleged Japanese war criminals at the International Military Tribunal.

on the construction of a new city hall projected to cost $4.3 million. By the end of the year, lumber from the frame of the old building had been sold for reuse in a veterans' housing project in Mattapan, and Lynners began to wonder if the money being spent on a new city hall might not have been better spent on housing. In the end, the structure cost $2.5 million and was ready for occupancy by September 1949. The fact that it

was built without a parking lot incensed many Lynners; the newspaper called it "the blunder of the half century."

Local 201 and the Cold War

By that time the postwar world was already an unsettled one. In June 1947, over President Truman's veto, Congress passed the Taft-Hartley Act, which essentially nullified the gains organized

Members of the Fifteenth Engineering Company of the U.S. Marine Corps Reserve, many of them World War II veterans who after the war had drilled weekly behind the city's old post office, marched through Central Square on August 21, 1950, on their way to trains for Camp LeJeune in North Carolina. After a year of basic training, a few of the 233-man company served in the Korean War, while most held stateside training jobs.

labor had made with the Wagner-Connery Act of 1935 by, among other things, banning closed or union shops, making union members liable for losses during strikes, and compelling union leaders to take oaths that they were not communists. In August 1948, in a highly publicized hearing before the House Un-American Activities Committee, Whittaker Chambers accused Alger Hiss of having been a member of the Communist Party when he was a high-ranking official in the U.S. State Department in the 1930s.

Then, the month that Lynn's new city hall was dedicated, Americans learned that the Soviets had successfully tested an atomic bomb. During the war, the Soviets had been allies, and Josef Stalin had been "Uncle Joe" to many Americans; General

Electric in Lynn had even accepted a contract from the Soviet government to manufacture equipment that would build the Dnieperstroy Dam. But by 1949, the Soviets, aggrieved by the Allied partition of European territory after the war, had suddenly become enemies, and communist infiltration had become a real issue to Americans. On June 25, 1950, the Korean conflict broke out, and before it ended four years later thirty-five Lynn men had been killed in action.

Concern about communism also had particular ramifications for the labor movement in Lynn. The issue of communist influence in Lynn unions had emerged in the 1920s and again in 1941 when Albert Fitzgerald, president and charter member of the union General Electric workers had

In 1953 Mayor Arthur Frawley and Lynn Fire Department Captain Ernest Williams stood in Central Square during an air raid drill. A fact of life during World War II, air raid drills were resumed during the Korean conflict.

set up in 1933, defeated James Carey in an election for the international presidency of the United Electrical Workers (UE). Carey had tried to pass a proposal to allow local unions to ban communists from holding offices, but most delegates to the UE convention were disaffected by Carey's management-friendly leadership and unconvinced that communism was a problem.

In 1948 the federal government stepped into the fray once more when the Atomic Energy Commission announced that it considered UE a security risk and thus refused to allow the union to represent any workers at General Electric's atomic energy plant, then being completed in Schenectady. The announcement was front-page news in Lynn. Anticommunism began to affect the CIO, which supported the anticommunist affidavits stipulated in the Taft-Hartley Act— affidavits many UE leaders in Lynn and elsewhere had refused to sign. By September 1949, UE had withdrawn from the CIO, and at the CIO's November convention it expelled UE and formed the International Union of Electrical Workers (IUE), which included those Lynners who believed the "left-wing influence" in Local 201 was too strong.

What followed over the next decade was an array of court actions and certification elections to settle whether Local 201's treasury and membership belonged to UE or IUE, actions that took place as the influence of unions declined overall. The number of labor organizations in Massachusetts had fallen by thirty-one between 1949 and 1950 and total membership by almost ten thousand. In 1950 Lynn still was home

▲ In August 1950 thousands of workers from the three General Electric plants in the city walked out and assembled on Lynn Common after maintenance workers had been locked out. Workers set up picket lines at River Works, West Lynn, and Allerton Street "within a matter of minutes," the newspaper reported, and struck the company for seventeen days. ▼

to forty-seven unions with 23,296 members, but the question of which union was the legitimate representative of workers' interests paralleled the continuing decline of organized labor; by 1980 Local 201 had eight thousand members, only half what it had in 1950.

During times of particular labor-management strife in the nation's history, claims that unions had been infiltrated and inspired by out-of-town leftist agitators had commonly been leveled: in 1924 Father Francis W. Maley of St. Joseph's Roman Catholic Church claimed in an issue of *Union Worker* that "a lot of bolshevik cranks" with support from the city's "foreigners" were sinking Lynn's shoe industry. But Local 201 was a homegrown union; most of its leaders and members had been living and working in Lynn all their lives. A hostile meeting of two thousand of the local's membership at Lynn City Hall was inconclusive on the UE-IUE question because many members, while acknowledging that there were communists within UE as a whole, were unconvinced that the local was dominated by "reds." By 1950 both unions represented GE workers. Still, IUE mounted a vigorous campaign to lure UE members into its local by suggesting that, in view of the government's reluctance to support the UE, the old union threatened the company's profitability and, hence, members' jobs. Certification elections in May 1950, August 1951, December 1953, and March 1960 consistently turned in IUE's favor. However, the margin between those who supported each union narrowed over the decade despite the fact that in 1953 Senator Joseph McCarthy himself came to Boston

to interrogate thirty of Lynn's "suspected Communists" in UE and Senator John F. Kennedy had publicly asserted that UE was a communist union. In November 1953 General Electric fired five employees, two of them in fact IUE members who invoked the Fifth Amendment under McCarthy's questioning. From that point on the company enforced a policy of firing those employees who admitted to being a communist or who could not clear themselves of charges that they were; by the time the policy was suspended in 1966, twenty-eight persons had been fired on account of it. And by that time UE and IUE both were much weaker, and workers at General Electric had splintered into at least twelve smaller unions.

Turning toward the Suburbs

Fear of communism and of nuclear devastation combined with other features of the postwar world to turn Americans inward. The GI Bill, signed into law by President Roosevelt in June 1944, guaranteed mortgages for veterans' first homes, and many returning servicemen were anxious to pick up life where they had left it off. Marriage and birth rates soared after the war; historian Elaine Tyler May has noted that the generation that came of age during and after the war was "the most marrying generation on record." Moreover, many servicemen had seen a harrowing

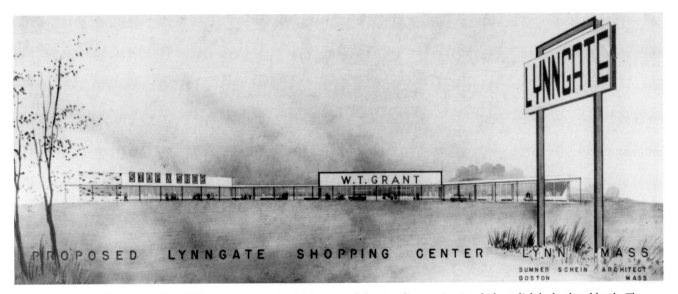

The Lynnway and other metropolitan highways encouraged suburban growth by spreading services into hitherto lightly developed lands. The Lynngate on Boston Street (on the site of the burned Agoos tannery) was among six new shopping centers that had opened on the North Shore by 1961. Photograph courtesy the Boston Herald.

In 1948 members of the Lynn family of Evelina Anderson assembled for a photograph in their home on Suffolk Street. Sitting on the floor in front are Janet and Barbara Anderson; in back of them on the couch are Audrey Anderson, Frances (Mrs. Sterling) Anderson, Pearl E. Anderson Brown holding her daughter Deborah, Avon Anderson, and Evelina. Standing in the rear are Sterling Anderson, E. Carlton Brown, and Frederick and Warren Anderson. Photograph courtesy Mr. and Mrs. E. Carlton Brown.

world in Europe and the Pacific, a devastation unparalleled in their experience, and the development of atomic power seemed to put the whole world at risk. As May has observed, the World War II generation "had grown up with emergency as a way of life."

As a consequence, home came to seem a haven, and spending for the home—forestalled first by the depression and then by the war—picked up at a stunning pace. Consumer spending rose 60 percent between 1945 and 1950, but spending on household furnishings increased 240 percent. The

postwar period was one in which the metered parking space replaced the train station and the television, more slowly, replaced going to the movies; in Lynn, both televisions and parking meters arrived on the scene in 1948. Every indication pointed toward increasing privacy and the corresponding need for single-family homes. "The idea was for everybody to have his own back yard and garden," former mayor Irving Kane once recalled. "American literature is replete with that post-World War II ideal." In the middle of 1945 "scores of modern homes" lined the extension of Childs Street that

In December 1958 Lynn architect Melvin Coombs designed a house for construction worker Sergio Grappi and his wife Dolores, which had been built at 53 Fay's Avenue in Lynn by 1966. Coombs designed houses throughout the North Shore between 1937 and 1973, but the bulk of them were built after World War II to accommodate a growing suburban population.

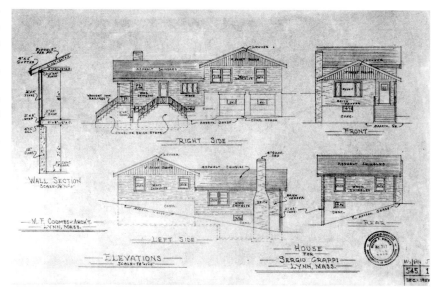

Lynn mothers took their children to Lynn Woods for a costumed May Day parade in the 1950s; the king for the day pulled a wagon carrying the group's lunches.

had just been built through Hill's field, long the city's old circus grounds and the site of many sports contests since about 1895. But in general Lynn, long hemmed in by the ocean and other towns, had very little room for single-home development.

Rent control during and after the war tended to visit neglect upon much of the existing housing stock, especially in neighborhoods close to downtown, and the fact that few buyers wanted the small multi-family houses that made up much of the Brickyard tended only to worsen the neglect and hasten the abandonment of the neighborhood by

those who could afford to move. "If you got any money at all you put lace curtains in your window and moved to East Lynn," city fireman Edward McDonald once recalled of the Irish American population in the area. After the war the city was set upon the first major outmigration it had ever experienced. By 1946, Kane noted, "Summer Circle, Laconia Court, had become almost totally depopulated" as families—many of them new ones about to usher in the baby boom—sought a suburban life. Outmigration also hurt such neighborhoods as Wyoma. "In the early 1940s there weren't many kids in the old neighborhood. Our generation had grown up and gone to war," Robert Dunning recalled. "When we came back, we produced the baby boom and the area became lousy with kids again in the 50s and 60s." But since the early 1960s, he noted, most of the people who had lived in the neighborhood before the war had moved out. "I don't know of a town within ten miles of Lynn which does not have an extraordinarily large ex-Lynn population," Kane noted in the late 1960s.

One aspect of the postwar world that accelerated the move away from Lynn and other cities was the development of interstate, urban arterial, and beltway highways. Instigated by federal legislation in 1944 designed partly to provide jobs for veterans, these highways had a withering effect on downtowns across the country as traffic was routed away from them. Route 128, once called

In 1956 Lynn Classical High School was full of students who had been born just before Pearl Harbor. Henry Dembowski, whose father Walter was then president of St. Michael's Polish National Alliance and a member of the city welfare board, was a senior when this view of him (with eyeglasses, seated at table) and other students was taken in the high school's lunchroom. Photograph courtesy Henry Dembowski.

145

In 1953, on the rotary near the heavily used Lynn Beach, Christie's and Roland's Ice Cream offered fried foods and ice cream to beachgoers. Patrons who finished Roland's huge banana bucket could have another for free, but few were still hungry after the first one. Also on the rotary was the Jack in the Box. After the MDC built the Lynnway, Christie's moved to the Jack in the Box location, and Roland's moved slightly back from the rotary. Photographs courtesy Metropolitan District Commission.

Though envisioned to support heavy industry on each side, the Lynnway rapidly became a corridor of automobile-oriented businesses—car dealerships, gas stations, drive-in restaurants, and car washes. One MDC traffic count in 1968 found that on an average weekday 38,850 cars traveled on the Lynnway, 5,000 more outbound than inbound.

By the beginning of 1960 the area including Summer, Harbor, Tremont, and Pleasant streets had been slated for urban renewal. The Summer Street view (below) shows a still active commercial district, while Harbor Street was lined with junkyards and well-worn frame residences. A neglected tenement sat across the street from St. Mary's Convent on Tremont Street (above right). The Boston Herald *photographer who shot these photographs noted that the thirty-five-acre area in which these properties stood was to become an "industrial park." Photographs courtesy the* Boston Herald.

the Circumferential Highway, had been planned to ring metropolitan Boston as early as 1930. Delayed by the depression and the war, the road's construction began in earnest after the war, and by 1954 scores of businesses had already moved, largely from urban areas, to the highway's suburban edges.

By 1947 the wheels that would turn to create the modern Lynnway were set in motion as well. Traffic through Lynn had increased greatly after the Sumner and Callahan tunnels had opened (the first in 1934, the second after the war), and one Civil Works Administration study that year had documented an extraordinary number of accidents at the intersection of Market and Broad streets. When in 1947 the state refused representative Norman E. Folsom's request that it build an extension to Market Street to end the severe traffic congestion, Folsom turned in 1950 to the Metropolitan District Commission. The Lynn Port Authority had been created to develop the land over which the highway would later run, but its plans for heavy industry there had come up short when surveys determined that factory buildings could not be built on the land, much

of it created in 1929 by filling. Between 1946 and 1962, the LPA sold or gave the land in its charge away to, among other entities, the MDC.

By August 1955 the multilane, divided Lynnway connected General Edwards Bridge with a new rotary at Nahant circle. The $3.6 million highway did solve the city's traffic problem, but it revived numerous development issues at the same time. General Electric's Lester W. Burton, chair of the Chamber of Commerce's community planning committee, declared that the Lynnway and the land bordering it was "Lynn's industrial frontier" and

147

that what the city did to develop the land would "set the standard for the future development and growth of the entire community." But despite a few nibbles, industrial development failed to occur along the Lynnway. Lynn was by then only weakly linked to materials and markets. Commercial traffic in the harbor had all but expired; only Hutchinson Lumber Company still received an occasional shipment (and in 1957 it successfully sued the commonwealth for having cut it off from its own wharf and harbor facilities when it created the Lynnway). Moreover, Boston and Maine freight and passenger service to and from Lynn had been sharply curtailed in the late 1950s and early 1960s.

On its way to becoming a gaudy commercial strip, the Lynnway also had many deteriorating structures and much vacant land along its borders, and by the 1960s both this area and the Brickyard had become targeted for urban renewal. The tract destined for demolition stretched along the northeast side of the Lynnway from Commercial to Pleasant streets and reached toward downtown Lynn as far as Market Street. The Brickyard still had many devoted residents, including many Italian families who owned homes and had developed their yards with gardens and outbuildings; Primo Lombardi, a salesman, restaurateur, and construction worker whose son Sam became a Lynn policeman, had dug a cellar by hand from beneath the Alley Street home he had purchased, had built a two-car garage, had installed a bocce court, and raised grapes, rabbits, and chickens in his back yard. In deference to the Brickyard's many defenders, some city officials had proposed "selective demolition"—that is, tearing down every other house

By April 1965 demolition in the urban renewal area was well underway. Lynn's H. S. Walker took these photographs of the wreckers at State and Pleasant streets (the Waldorf Theater is in the foreground above) and at the northwest corner of Pleasant and Summer streets.

to create larger lots, but the idea apparently fell on deaf ears; nearly the entire area was targeted for demolition by 1961.

Urban renewal was designed to extend as well to a twenty-three-acre site at Market and Tremont streets, but as demolition proceeded a group that called itself Citizens for a Better Lynn organized to stop the project at Commercial Street. CBL, according to member and later mayor Antonio Marino, was dedicated to keeping the downtown from becoming "nothing but empty fields." Marino, who had grown up in the neighborhood, thought of the Brickyard as "the Quincy

Market of its time" and watched with dismay as the neighborhood's meat and fish markets, produce stores and delicatessens, bakeries and barber shops were destroyed. Urban renewal was, in his view, "really a bloodbath" that undercut the city's tax base at a time when much of its downtown factory space was empty.

Lynn and the Civil Rights Movement

The postwar years also gave rise to the first broad-based efforts to enact federal civil rights protections since the post-Civil War constitutional amendments and the Civil Rights Act of 1875. Historians suggest the roots of civil rights activism lay in the Second World War, first in the massive population shift of rural African American people to the urban North. In 1941 African American labor leader A. Philip Randolph, who had promised a massive march on Washington on behalf of unemployed African Americans seeking defense work, forced President Franklin D. Roosevelt's hand and helped assure creation of the Fair Employment Practices Committee. Roosevelt's executive order in May 1943 calling for mandatory nondiscrimination clauses in defense contracts and subcontracts directly sparked the Detroit and Harlem riots of 1943—and demonstrated that racism and racial discrimination were national, not sectional, issues. Even though the Senate killed efforts to make the FEPC permanent

in 1946, 1950, and 1952, by 1946 five states including Massachusetts had enacted fair employment practice acts.

After the war, the return of more than one million African American veterans added energy to the dawning effort to assure that civil rights existed at home. These citizens had seen cultures in which racism seemed not to exist as well as ones in which individual rights were routinely and egregiously abused; like African American veterans of earlier wars, they also felt entitled to more than second-class status after having served their country. In 1946 the federal branch of the U.S. government took its first civil rights action in more than seventy years when the Supreme Court ruled that segregation on interstate transportation was unconstitutional. And in 1948 President Harry Truman desegregated the U.S. armed forces.

The beginnings of civil rights activism in Lynn probably date to the war years, although African Americans in the city had organized the Lynn Association for the Advancement of Colored People (not then affiliated with the National Association for the Advancement of Colored People, or NAACP) in 1930 and again in 1939; the earlier chapter, founded by Horace Harmon, Edward W. Brown, Cam Moore, and others, met at Association Hall on Groveland Street, a gathering place for African American families, who numbered roughly two hundred in this decade. The 1939 chapter was

Mayor Thomas Costin joined Lynn's chapter of the National Association for the Advancement of Colored People in March 1959. S. Matthew Carrington gave Costin his membership certificate as Zion Baptist Church Rev. Toussaint Davis looked on.

started by Dr. William Washington, E. Carleton Brown, and others and met at 17 Beach Street.

During the war Lynn began to see its first notable migration of African Americans from the South in many decades. Some were servicemen stationed in the area. The influx of southern families, many of whom expected not to encounter racism and discrimination in the North, helped spark civil rights efforts in the city. A more direct motivation took place in 1943. Barbara Smith and Helen Green, local African American women, had sought to enter the nurses' training program at Lynn Hospital only to be denied entrance. Dr. Vernon Carter exposed the situation, and though he was unsuccessful in changing the hospital's decision (Smith and Green both trained in other cities and spent their careers as nurses and nursing instructors), the event gave rise five years later to Lynn's first NAACP chapter, created in May 1948 by Robert Berry, Abner Darby, Virginia Barton, Edward Battle, Dave McCoy, Sr., Francis Gatley, and others.

Lynn civil rights activism was given substantial encouragement by the visits of Martin Luther King, Jr., to the city in the early 1950s. King, who had come to Boston from his native Georgia in 1951 to study for his doctorate in theology at Boston University, came to Lynn frequently on Sundays at the invitation of Ernest L. Savory, Jr., a Lynn native who was living in Boston and had been a member of the fraternity Alpha Phi Alpha as a student at Ohio State University. Savory was King's fraternity big brother and brought him home to 368 Summer Street in Lynn for his mother's Sunday dinners. "He always said he just wanted to go home and help people," Savory later told the *Lynn Item.* "Not just my people, just people."

In 1954, as King was finishing his doctoral work in Boston, the U.S. Supreme Court ruled in *Brown vs. Board of Education of Topeka* that the "separate but equal" ruling of an earlier court, in *Plessy v. Ferguson* of 1896, was unconstitutional. The efforts to create equal access to public education gathered steam as the court in 1955 extended the segregation ban to other public facilities. In that year as well, the murder of the African American teenager Emmett Till and the refusal of Rosa Parks to give up her bus seat to a white passenger in Montgomery, Alabama, galvanized African Americans North and South, as well as white Americans interested in the cause of civil rights.

In 1963 eleven Lynners joined some two hundred thousand other white and African Americans in the march "for jobs and freedom" on Washington. Abner Darby, who had moved to Lynn from Texas, was among them, as was Ethel Young, who had grown up in Lynn and worked at the Lynn Public Library. Rev. Edgar D. Romig, Rev. Arthur F. Kimber, Jr., Rev. Norman Zane Knoy,

In 1956 employees of Burrows and Sanborn's department store, in business in Lynn since 1897, gathered for a reunion at the Hotel Edison. Several African American women were among them, and in the postwar years the city's population of African American people was the highest it had ever been.

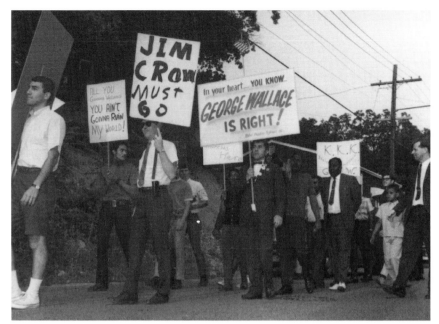

In July 1968 members of the city's NAACP branch staged a peaceful demonstration during the visit of presidential aspirant George C. Wallace of Alabama. Protesters did not themselves protest against the counterdemonstration of Polish freedom fighter Josef Mlot-Mroz, shown at center in the bowtie. Abner Darby, president of the Lynn NAACP chapter, is in front of the last sign. Photograph courtesy Lynn Daily Evening Item.

Rev. Early W. Eldridge, Rev. J. Herman Freemand and his wife, Ann Bennett, William Robinson, Ralph Tyler, and others were part of the historic march and heard King's "I Have a Dream" address. The march directly influenced the passage of the 1964 Civil Rights Act and the 1965 Voting Rights Act, the first federal laws to prohibit discrimination in almost a century. In Lynn, the local NAACP chapter conducted frequent drives to gather money and clothing in direct aid to those activists in the South whose livelihoods were threatened by their protest, and one member, Edward Battle, was sent south to work in the hostile climate of voter registration drives.

The local chapter also continued to work in support of changing segregative practices in Lynn, where few factories hired African Americans for any job except foundry work and where some stores refused to hire them at all. In the late 1960s the chapter worked with General Electric to create the Step Program, a skilled training course for minorities, and with North Shore Community College to create the Motivation to Education Program. This latter project works with minority youth who are not motivated to continue their educations to keep them in school; it exists to this day.

At about the same time, local NAACP members organized a peaceful protest during the July 1968 visit to the city of presidential aspirant George

C. Wallace of Alabama. Darby, president of the chapter, and treasurer Charles Harris criticized the local park commission's decision to permit Wallace to speak at the city-owned Briarcliff Lodge on Sluice Pond. "I think it is time Lynn officials listened to what the people of Lynn want," Harris told the newspaper after having received hundreds of calls objecting to the decision to let Wallace speak at Briarcliff. "The Park Commission is paying no attention. Thousands of people don't want this." Park Commission chair John J. McManus asserted that the commission had no legal right to refuse Wallace's request, and alleged threats against park commission members and their families compelled local police to strengthen police protection of Wallace during his July 8 address. As two hundred people (including Lynn public assistance director Edmund McCarthy and Lynn attorney Charles Ingram) picketed outside the lodge, Wallace used the occasion to extend his traditional assaults on gun control, on the failure of law and order in the United States, on communists, and on liberals in general. "If I am successful," he told the crowd of five hundred in Lynn, "I will come back and help shake the eye teeth of the liberals in Massachusetts and the United States." In Lynn, the contest over Wallace's appearance resulted in the appointment of local labor leader David McCoy, Sr., as the first African American member of the park commission.

In 1927 Champion Lamp, which had started business in Danvers in 1900, took over the vacant Lynnway factory of the A. M. Creighton Shoe Company, claimed to be the most modern shoe factory in the world when it was built in 1922 but almost immediately beset by labor disputes. Champion made incandescent and, by 1939, fluorescent lamps and was thought to be the largest privately owned lamp producer in the country before the Marsh family sold the business to International Telephone and Telegraph Corporation in 1966. The Lynnway factory, used as a Norelco plant for many years, was eventually acquired by West Lynn Creamery and put into service as an auxiliary warehouse.

For some African Americans who had come to Lynn from the South, however, the NAACP chapter did not seem to be moving fast or far enough. An alternative civil rights group, the Gaylords, was created to take more militant action, and the gulf between older African Americans raised in the North and newer families was evident also in the increasing number of Pentecostal churches in the city and in the tendency to view East Lynn as the home of more established families and West Lynn as the home of newer and less affluent ones. This rift, combined with the influx of black and white Latinos from Central America and the West Indies after immigration laws were relaxed in 1965, moved local African Americans, whites, and Latinos to create the Community Minority Cultural Center in 1971. In part to avoid being identified with either the west or east side of the city and in part to call attention to the pressing social and economic need of inner-city residents, the organization sited itself downtown and began to address itself both to the values of multiculturalism and to the social service and economic issues of greater Lynn's minority residents. The CMCC also implements programs aimed at reducing violence in the city's downtown and at reviving the center

By 1977 Lynn Realty Trust Building #4 was both a shoe outlet and vacant space. In 1980 only several hundred people still worked in Lynn's shoe industry.

In 1981, just before the November 28 fire, Lynn photographer Peter Bates photographed women workers at Benson Shoe Company, then Lynn's largest shoe factory.

shops in the city, and by 1980 even fewer jobs remained in an industry that had once employed many thousands.

Even though more than half of the local work force still had manufacturing jobs by 1974, unemployment in Lynn had reached 12 percent that year, higher than it was at both the state and national levels. General Electric still garnered defense contracts, and in August 1965 a fuel cell built at the River Works powered the Gemini 5 spacecraft in its nine-day orbit around the earth. The cell used reactions between fuel and oxygen to create enough electrical energy to propel the craft through 120 orbits and produced drinkable water as a byproduct; it was the first spaceborne use of fuel cell technology. But even as a billboard atop Building 88 proclaimed Lynn as "Turbo-Town" and birthplace of the American jet engine, the company had suffered some downturn since the end of the war: in 1956 its street lighting and motor divisions were transferred out of Lynn, which caused a heavy loss of jobs. By 1975 local unemployment climbed to nearly 20 percent. By 1977 scarcely more than one thousand people worked in the eight structures Lynn Realty Trust had built between 1903 and 1915 to house more than five thousand shoe workers, and much of the eight hundred thousand square feet they offered stood empty.

The 1981 Fire
Four years later Lynn's second great fire ended the vacancy problem by burning almost all of these factories down. On November 28, 1981—ninety-two years and two days after the city's first great fire—fire broke out in the eight-story brick building at 264–66 Broad Street, the longtime home of Oxford Shoe Company and the second building Lynn Realty Trust had put up, in 1906. The city had been in the process of tearing the old building down as part of a plan to rehabilitate the area, and the sprinkler system had been shut off. At 2:35 on the morning of November 28, two policemen noticed flames in the building, which was already unstable because its rear wall had been demolished. Twenty-two minutes later, Lynn firefighters officially declared the fire to be out of control and spreading. Firefighters from eighty

city, increasingly abandoned by businesses and middle-class homeowners.

By the time the civil rights movement was visibly active in Lynn, the city's downtown had fallen on hard times as the local shoe industry continued to decline. By 1950 New England produced only 32 percent of the nation's footwear, a 30 percent loss since the century began. At the time about 2,200 Lynners worked at twenty-five shoe firms in Lynn, but in the 1960s a sharp increase in shoe imports from Europe and Asia and the growing use of synthetic leather dealt the industry another bruising blow. Almost a symbol of the industry's decline, Huntt's Central Square cafe, the former "Crispin's Congress," closed its doors in 1960, and by 1965 only twenty-one factories were left in Lynn. A decade later, only 450 people were working in just eight shoe companies all over the region were called in to assist; seven hundred fought the fire in all.

By the time the fire was under control more than fifteen hours later, eighteen industrial buildings had been completely destroyed and eight others were heavily or seriously damaged. Lynn's crowded industrial district, an artifact of a time when nearly everyone walked to work, had made the fire much harder to contain. According to Joseph Scanlon, chief of the Lynn Fire Department at the time, the narrow alleys between the tall structures acted as vortices that concentrated heat, flame, and "superheated" air and channeled it along Broad Street. The street lost nine buildings, including numbers 264–66, 244 (Walter Dyer Leather and Colonial Wood Heel), 278 (housing Oxford Hopkins, Elliott Morris Company, Colonial Bag, and Northeast Cutting Die), 190 (Benson Shoe, then Lynn's largest shoe shop), 278 (Elm Shank and Heel), and 176 (Sam's Grille). Four additional buildings on Washington Street (including J. Sanger Attwill's furniture factory, vacated only weeks before), one on the Lynnway, and one on Farrar Street were total losses.

For weeks the acres of rubble left on the site smoldered, and among the fallen and snow-covered debris fires spontaneously erupted until December 14, when firefighters finally declared the blaze "all out." The 1981 fire had burned over part of the same area the 1889 fire had consumed, had caused injury to eight Lynn and two out-of-town firefighters, and had caused a loss of eighty million dollars. At the request of Governor Edward King President Ronald Reagan declared Lynn a major disaster area, and to many Lynners it certainly was. The 1889 fire had burned a much larger part of the city, but the shoe industry had been able to rebuild itself afterward. But after the 1981 fire it could not. In a much more forceful way than the slow transition of the economy had compelled other Americans to realize, the fire forced Lynners to look away from a future in which manufacturing held the greatest promise.

The November 28, 1981, fire burned over some of the same area that the city's first great conflagration had consumed in 1889. The 1981 blaze took more than fifteen hours to control and involved more than seven hundred area firefighters.

On November 30, 1981, Lynn Fire Department Chief Joseph Scanlon described the course of the fire to Senators Edward Kennedy and Paul Tsongas as they walked through the ruins of the fire with Mayor Antonio Marino. The city was declared a major disaster area, and the fire's cause was never discovered. Photograph courtesy the Boston Herald.

During Lynn's 1950 centennial the Queen's Court promoted the event as they cavorted in the surf at Lynn Beach. From left are Marie Bergen, Barbara Newman, Barbara O'Shaughnessy, and Barbara Fillion, all between eighteen and twenty-one years old at the time. Photograph courtesy the Boston Herald.

Just one week before the United States sent troops to fight in Korea, Lynn celebrated its centennial as a city with a series of events between June 11 and 17, 1950. A huge parade marched along Union, Munroe, and Market streets past the reviewing stand at Lynn's new city hall. Parade participants were photographed as they prepared their huge balloon to float above the event. The week also featured the first flight of a jet airplane over the city. Photograph courtesy Bob Furlong, Lynn City Hall.

Local celebrity Walking Mike Doyle entertained the staff of the Lynn Telegram-News during a restaurant dinner in the 1940s. For the Fifth Liberty Loan during World War I, Doyle had walked 485 miles from Lynn to Washington to announce the city's subscription personally; it took him ten days. In late January of 1946 he arrived in the city after having walked 3,200 miles from Los Angeles. Doyle's walks were legendary, and between the wars he often walked long distances for sports causes, such as the construction of Lynn's municipal stadium in 1928.

155

In 1952 the youthful Congressman John F. Kennedy visited Lynn during his campaign for the United States Senate. Kennedy was greeted by two supporters—future mayor Patsy Caggiano and Theresa Parascondola, a popular street vendor known to generations of Lynners as the "Balloon Lady." Her father, "Pete the Lobster," was also a well-known vendor. Photograph courtesy Vincent O'Brien.

Partly because of such athletes as Jim Hegan and Harry Agganis, Lynn had always been a popular spot among Boston Red Sox players. In 1946 the club began a Class B farm team, the Lynn Tigers, which won three consecutive pennants before being sold in 1949 and moved to Marblehead. Johnny Pesky, Oregon-born Red Sox infielder from 1942 to 1952, married Ruth Hickey of Lynn and became the city's adopted son. Pesky worked out at the city's Jewish Community Center and played in the World Series against the St. Louis Cardinals in 1946.

Harry Agganis (at right) had been a star baseball player at Lynn Classical High School in 1947 when he was named the outstanding high school football player in eastern Massachusetts. Son of a Lynn produce dealer, Agganis went on to Boston University and then to the Boston Red Sox, where he played first base. On July 27, 1955, he was batting .313 after the twenty-fifth game of his second season when he suddenly died, at the age of twenty-five, of a pulmonary embolism. His funeral at St. George's Greek Orthodox Church (below) was one of Lynn's largest. At the coffin his nephew Michael holds a trophy the sports star had won in 1950 and had earlier promised the boy; with Michael is Louis Pappas of Chicago, Agganis's maternal uncle. On opening day of the 1956 season the Red Sox left first base open in Agganis's honor as they took the field, and the city of Boston renamed the street leading to Boston University's Nickerson Field Agganis Way in 1995. Red Sox photograph courtesy Bob Keaney.

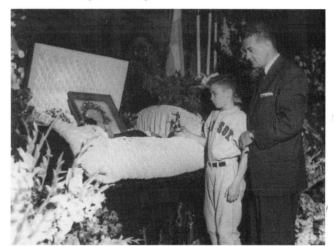

The Lynn Boys Club boxing team competed in the New England finals in 1955. From left are longtime Boys Club boxing coach Tony Pavone, Fran Wall, Richard Woodworth, Bernard Ouelette, and Al Doucette.

Lynn's "Salute to Youth" parade on August 9, 1975 drew a crowd of 125,000 spectators and featured twenty-three drum and bugle corps and eighteen color guards. The Jean-ettes, shown here, had just taken third place among all-girl corps at the World Open Drum and Bugle Corps Championships at Everett Memorial Stadium.

Perhaps inspired by the success of such teams as the Cornet and Fraser All-Stars and Classical High's 1946 football team, which won the national schoolboy football crown at the Orange Bowl that year, companies and stores throughout the city sponsored ball teams and bowling teams. Jack's Lunch at the corner of Chatham and Marianna streets in East Lynn was among many teams— including the Senators, the Pioneers, the Coffee-Boilers, the Tacomas, and the Iroquois—who played amateur ball. Town Taxi at 53 Central Avenue sponsored its own bowling team (below) in 1951.

Amateur sport of all kinds was also popular in postwar Lynn. At the corner of Essex and Stewart streets near Cogan's Corner variety store, Raymond A. Russell posed with his soapbox racer.

In 1951, the first year the city fielded little league teams, Lynn boys won the state championships. The team posed at the end of the season with Mayor Stuart Tarr and a bunch of proud adults, probably parents. Photograph courtesy Lynn Public Library.

In the 1950s Lynn native and Cleveland Indians catcher Jim Hegan posed with several of the city's retailers. Harry S. Goldstein had been in business in Lynn as Henry the Hatter since 1935 and had been making caps in the city since 1925. Hegan played for the Indians from 1941 to 1957 and then for four other major league clubs before his retirement in 1960. He died in Swampscott in 1984.

As the Metropolitan District Commission prepared to create a much larger Lynnway, its planners took interior and exterior photographs of nearly every structure along the road. During the noon hour on October 29, 1954, they photographed inside Varley's Diner at 661 Broad Street. Opened in 1940 by Edith C. Varley, the diner was an immensely popular after-the-movies spot, and its hot fudge sundaes were highly regarded. In the 1950s William Argeros owned the diner, which closed in 1974. Photograph courtesy Metropolitan District Commission.

Lynners frequented several fish and chip shops, such as Charlie and Bob's (now Hayward's) on Lynnfield Street and Arnold's Fish and Chips Shop on Western Avenue between Chatham Street and Eutaw Avenue. Proprietor Ernest Arnold had served in the Army during World War II and opened the shop immediately afterward; it did business at this location until 1969.

In 1952, at the height of the Korean conflict, Lynn's Richard G. Fecteau (above center) was declared missing. In November 1954 Lynners learned that Chinese communists had sentenced Fecteau to twenty years' solitary confinement at Green Basket prison in Peking on the charge that he was a spy. Fecteau and another man, later confirmed to be a CIA agent, had been shot down over Manchuria in the midst of a secret mission. In January 1958 Fecteau's mother flew to China to urge her son's release, but he was not freed until December 12, 1971. A former Classical High and Boston University football player, Fecteau became assistant athletic director at Boston University in 1977. Photograph courtesy Vincent O'Brien.

On November 29, 1956, Lynn watched as the wooden and vacant Agoos tannery near the entrance to Pine Grove Cemetery went up in flames. Originally the G. K. Pevear Company and one of the largest leather plants in the nation, the building had been sold by Pevear's heirs in 1916 to Lassar Agoos, head of Agoos Leather Company in Boston. The Lynn factory had closed two months before the fire and the sprinkler system had been dismantled, but the fire department had not been notified. The flames spread to the walls and sills, saturated with leather dust, and quickly engulfed the building because its doors and windows had also been removed. The fire destroyed five buildings before nearly three hundred firefighters from five towns brought it under control. The building was then one of the oldest in the city. Photograph courtesy the Boston Herald.

Jesse Gunn Payette was an entertainer of considerable reputation in Lynn and surrounding communities from the 1920s through the early 1960s. For many years she played organ at the Strand (later the Warner) Theater. This photograph of her and her ensemble was probably taken in the late 1950s.

Still a vibrant part of Lynn, the city's Greek American community laid the cornerstone for a new edifice for St. George's church at 54 South Common Street in 1953.

161

In early September 1954 the crews of
Lynn Gas and Electric assembled in
the company yard as they prepared to
clean up from Hurricane Carol. The
storm packed the fastest winds ever
recorded in Lynn—eighty-six miles per
hour, a mile per hour faster than the
hurricane of 1938. Less than two weeks
later Hurricane Edna struck the city,
and in mid-August 1955 Hurricane
Diane gave Lynn a record 12.59-inch
rainfall. It was a hard decade for
weather: in 1956 three blizzards hit
the North Shore in eight days, and on
Valentines Day 1958 another one left
19.4 inches, the largest snowfall in
a single day in Lynn.

On January 6, 1959, Woolworth's
five-and-ten-cent store on Market
and Liberty streets burned; a Lynn
Fire Department pumper shows the
aftereffects of fighting the fire in
frigid weather.

By 1969 General Electric employees were affiliated
with at least thirteen separate unions. That winter,
these unions banded together to stage a strike that
lasted 101 days and ended February 4, 1970. It was the
longest in GE's history. Company officials claimed the
strike was largely fruitless because workers after the
strike accepted the wage increase the company had proposed beforehand. Yet the union won its effort to tie
wages to the cost of living, which especially in the
inflationary 1970s meant more to workers than general
raises. GE also agreed to new contract provisions on
sick pay, vacation, contract expiration date, and skilled
trade wage rates. The AFL-CIO supported a boycott of
company products during the strike, and in 1970 the
U.S. Supreme Court charged GE with violations of the
Taft-Hartley Act for its management of the strike.

162

On March 25, 1960, the federal National Labor Relations Board conducted another certification election in the decade-long struggle between United Electrical Workers and the CIO-affiliated International United Electrical Workers. UE had signed up more than 70 percent of River Works employees before the election, but IUE charged that its rival had planned "a program of work stoppages designed to sabotage this country's defense program." With support of Senators John F. Kennedy and Hubert Humphrey, IUE won certification again but by its narrowest margin ever—just 269 votes. Photograph courtesy the Boston Public Library, Print Department.

In October 1960 IUE staged a nationwide walkout of General Electric in order to win a thirty-five-hour work week for forty hours of pay. Strike tactics turned ugly: workers dumped molasses on the streets and threw tacks on top to puncture the tires of any car that attempted to cross the picket line into the factory. Union employee relations manager Bob Burns tried to scrape the tacks up, and one worker devised a magnetic chain attachment connected to his car's battery to sweep the tacks away. The strike ended quickly, and IUE abandoned its drive for fewer hours. Photograph courtesy the Boston Herald.

Lynn Beach continued to be a popular summer spot; this photograph of the crowded beach was taken in June 1960. Photograph courtesy the Boston Herald.

In 1973 retirees picketed General Electric to protest unsatisfactory pension benefits.

On January 21, 1961, the northern end of the Lynnway was flooded in a winter storm, cutting off access to Nahant. Photograph courtesy the Boston Herald.

In the 1960s members of Lynn's Boys Club gathered at the snack bar. After 1959 Lynn boys could also spend part of the summer at Creighton Pond Camp, a three-hundred-acre wooded tract with a pond in Middleton that Mr. and Mrs. Albert M. Creighton had given to the club. Albert Creighton had been one of the directors of the club when it revived and opened on Liberty Street in 1903.

Keeping up with the times and no doubt also trying to keep business downtown, Farber's shoe store on Market Street sponsored a promotion that gave one boy a spacesuit in about 1960. Mayor Thomas Costin (seated) and Irving Farber (standing behind him) are shown with the winning family.

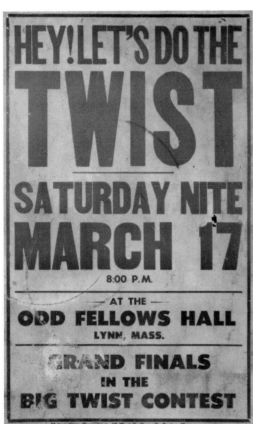

In August 1960 Ruth and Maurice Dinerman posed proudly with their staff on the opening day of the Holland Bakery in McDonough Square. Photograph courtesy North Shore Jewish Historical Society.

In 1962, when the International Order of Odd Fellows sponsored this dance, the Twist was the most popular novelty dance in the country. The fad started with Chubby Checker's "The Twist," the fourth best-selling song on the rhythm and blues charts in 1960, continued into 1961 with smash hit "Peppermint Twist," and was still going strong in 1962 with the Isley Brothers' "Twist and Shout." Within two years, the Beatles would make "Twist and Shout" popular all over again. This Lynn dance probably took place at Glenmere Lodge on Maple Street.

Between 1919 and 1970 not a single decade of professional baseball had passed without a Lynn man among its players. Born in Revere, Anthony Richard (Tony) Conigliaro had grown up in Lynn and had made it to the Boston Red Sox by 1964; the next year he led the American League with thirty-two home runs. In May 1967 Conigliaro (rear center) worked out with the Shore League Red Sox, but at the end of August that year he was hit in the face by a fastball at Fenway Park; the injury nearly ended his career. The Sox traded him to the California Angels in 1971, though he returned to play twenty-one games as a Red Sox in the 1975 season. Conigliaro's brother Billy also played for the Red Sox, the Milwaukee Brewers, and the Oakland Athletics between 1969 and 1973.

On February 23, 1965, Lynn police participated in the capture of accused Boston Strangler Albert DeSalvo, who had escaped from Bridgewater State Hospital to Lynn and had spent the night before in a cellar in a Western Avenue home. DeSalvo had gone to Simons uniform store to call his lawyer and give himself up. He was later murdered in prison. The strangler's second victim had been Helen Blake, a sixty-five-year-old nurse found strangled in her Newhall Street apartment in Lynn on April 3, 1962.

In 1976 the intersection of Summer and Commercial streets stood just on the edge of the urban renewal area; the vacant lots at the bottom of this bird's eye view show where structures had been cleared. General Electric's West Lynn Works is in the center background; Caggiano Towers, an elderly housing complex, is in the background at right.

Rock and roll really came to Lynn on a rainy June 24, 1966, when the Rolling Stones gave a concert at Manning Bowl. The three-year-old group was already a global sensation when Swampscott's Robert Walker managed to book Lynn as the group's first stop on its U.S. tour. Somehow during the short concert chaos broke out, fans charged the stage, and police used tear gas on the excited crowd. Fans and police argued about why tear gas was used for weeks afterward. Photograph courtesy Lynn Daily Evening Item.

While urban renewal razed most of the Brickyard, fire took other of the city's older structures. In January 1976 fire destroyed the 1873 First Universalist Church on Nahant Street.

The city lost other landmarks in the postwar period. The elaborate Broad Street fire station had stood on its lot for a century before a wrecking ball began to take it down at the end of April 1978.

Not all of old Lynn had disappeared by the 1970s, however. In 1974 Osborne's bird and seed store occupied what was originally a dwelling in Greek Revival style at the corner of Oxford and Washington streets. The building also served for a time as a lawyer's office.

By the mid-1970s, with the effects of urban renewal and the Lynnway clear to everyone, city officials sought to revive downtown Lynn through a variety of plans. One was the Union Street pedestrian walkway, built in 1977 and modeled on a successful mall built in Baltimore. However, with cars and buses banned, trade declined in many stores; Burrows and Sanborn and T. W. Rogers Company, both longtime features of downtown Lynn, both closed; so too did the mall itself, in 1985.

On September 11, 1971, a crowd of some three hundred supporters of the Progressive Labor party and other organizations marched from Central Square to General Electric's West Lynn plants to protest proposed layoffs and wage freezes. By the 1970s, Lynn's ethnic makeup had begun to change again with a new influx of Caribbean peoples, whose emigration had been favored by the relaxation of immigration law in 1965. Photograph courtesy the Boston Herald.

In advance of a public hearing about the proposed relocation of residents of the Brickyard's Summer Circle residents during the second phase of urban renewal, Mrs. Joan Lee meets with members of the Lynn Redevelopment Authority and the Citizens Advisory Committee on Urban Development as they toured the soon-to-be-demolished neighborhood in July 1965. From left are the Rev. Paul V. Donovan of St. Mary's Church, a member of the citizens committee; Winifred Jackson, a social worker on the redevelopment authority's relocation staff; James O'Neil, LRA relocation director; Mrs. Lee; and Walter T. McLeod, Jr., executive director of LRA.

Sally Schier wearing a St. Pius V School uniform escorts her younger sister Elaine to an audience with Santa Claus at the Police Woman's Benevolent Association Christmas Party held at the Oxford Club about 1949. Photograph courtesy Stephen Schier.

The February 1978 blizzard dumped twenty-seven inches of snow in Lynn and shut the city down for days. On February 7 Lynn Item photographer Walter Hoey caught a lone pedestrian walking down Exchange Street as the snowstorm fell; the next day, the snow over, highway crews managed to clear one lane each way on the Lynnway. The city mustered into service auxiliary policemen, two of whom patroled Munroe Street at night on February 10. Three days later sidewalks still were not cleared, as this photograph by the Lynn Public Library shows. Hoey photograph courtesy Lynn Daily Evening Item.

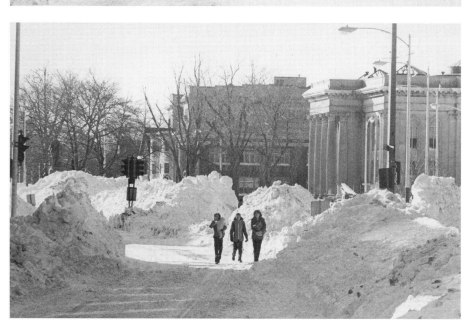

Five former mayors of Lynn— from left, Irving E. Kane, David L. Phillips, Thomas Costin, Stuart A. Tarr, and J. Warren Cassidy— sat together at the inauguration of Mayor Antonio Marino at Lynn City Hall in January 1978. Tarr had been mayor from 1948 to 1951, when the city's first public housing was built. Costin, longtime city postmaster and a candidate for U.S. Postmaster General due to his early support for John F. Kennedy, served as mayor from 1956 to 1961; urban renewal was initiated in his term. Kane, an attorney, was mayor from 1966 to 1969, during which urban renewal continued; Cassidy succeeded him for a one-year term, as did Phillips from 1974 to 1975. Behind Cassidy sat Eugene S. Dooley, superintendent of the Lynn Park Department.

In 1971, a year before becoming the city's first African American elected official in nearly a century (in 1886, Willis Browning had served on the city council) with his election to the school board, Vincent Jarvis was one of five General Electric employees in the country to receive the Gerald L. Phillippe Award for distinguished public service from Governor Francis Sargent. Born in Lynn in 1909, Jarvis began working at GE during World War II and was an engine assembler in the Aircraft Engine Group when he received the award. A graduate of English High, Jarvis was among the founders of Lynn Community Brotherhood, Inc., in the early 1950s and was on the board of the North Shore Branch of the Massachusetts Commission against Discrimination.

In 1971 city firefighters worked ten-hour days and fourteen-hour night shifts. That winter they took a plea to the polls to shorten their hours and won a reduction from a forty-eight- to a forty-two-hour work week. However, when Mayor Warren Cassidy offered the firefighters rotating eight-hour shifts and insisted they work every weekend, the firemen struck. By June Cassidy agreed to restore the old shifts. Shown left to right are Chief Joseph Scanlon, Jr., Thomas Upton, and Victor Ahern.

On election night 1972 Brickyard native Walter J. Boverini (left) celebrated his election to the state senate with his wife Christine and Thomas W. McGee, also a Brickyarder and then Speaker of the Massachusetts House of Representatives. McGee, who served longer as Speaker of the House than anyone else in the state's history, was elected to the House in 1962 and used Bill's Lunch in McDonough Square, shown below in the 1950s, as his unofficial office. The lunchroom operated at this site from 1943 to 1979. Boverini photograph courtesy Walter J. Boverini; Bill's Lunch photograph courtesy Les Matthews.

The Scangas family began West Lynn Creamery in 1938 as an ice cream stand; by 1991 it was the city's third largest employer with seven hundred persons. The creamery is one of the state's largest milk handling firms, and its Richdale products are distributed over much of the Northeast. Photograph courtesy Lynn Daily Evening Item.

In June 1971, as unemployment climbed in the city, a group of mothers from Lynn picketed in front of the State House in Boston over a delay in issuing welfare funds. Photograph courtesy the Boston Herald.

Lynn's ocean beach closed often in the 1970s because of high coliform bacteria counts, perhaps induced by current flowing from the city's outfall sewer, constructed in 1928. The system had piped sewage across Lynn Harbor to some distance off the Nahant headlands, but a storm in March 1931 closed Shirley Gut in Winthrop and redirected the current back toward shore. Despite frequent closings, King's Beach was often crowded when it was open. The Item's Bob Crosby photographed the beach on July 23, 1975.

On December 19, 1980, leather manufacturer Walter Dyer announced that he would drop fifteen hundred one-dollar bills from his brother's airplane one-half mile north of Lynn Hospital. He expected the wind to waft the bills into Central Square, where three thousand people waited hopefully to grab them. Dyer's plan fizzled when instead the wind took the money out to sea. Photograph courtesy Lynn Daily Evening Item.

The first Arab nations' embargo of U.S. oil supplies took place in 1973, and gasoline shortages plagued service station owners and motorists throughout much of the remaining decade. Donald Ellis, nephew of Harry W. Dill, Jr., owner of the Glenmere Shell station on Chestnut Street, apologized to customers when his supplies ran out in 1978; the station is no longer in business. Photograph courtesy Joseph Gavrain, Jr.

By 1978 Egg Rock was a barren island bearing no evidence of its former lighthouse and keeper's house. Lynn Item photograph by Jim Wilson.

173

By the early 1980s pollution control programs had helped make the ocean at Lynn's doorstep once more suitable for swimming, as these children jumping from the seawall demonstrated. Several serious injuries to seawall divers, however, compelled the Metropolitan District Commission to curb the practice.

Chapter 7

Modern Lynn

At the time of the 1981 fire more than 37 percent of the working-age population of Lynn was employed in manufacturing. As the percentage of Massachusetts workers in manufacturing declined steadily in the postwar years, Lynners managed to hang on to the city's traditional economy as global events seemed to guarantee a continued role for the United States military. Through the 1980s defense contracts continued to comprise about 70 percent of General Electric's work; the company manufactured the F404 engine and the F-117A stealth fighter, used in both Korea and Vietnam, and Lynn-made engines powered eleven different aircraft and five helicopters used in the Persian Gulf war. By 1991 River Works employed eight thousand people.

But even as early as 1954 it was clear that Lynn stood outside the general trend. By that year one state study showed that a greater percentage of the state's labor force (just short of 55 percent) worked in such service fields as transportation, government, communications, health, education, utilities, and wholesale and retail trade; a little less than 43 percent remained in manufacturing. By the late 1970s 67 percent of all New England workers were part of the service economy, and by 1990 hospitals were the biggest employers in the state. While manufacturing employment decreased between 1958 and 1978, employment in service trades more than doubled in those two decades.

Massachusetts Governor Michael Dukakis came to General Electric's River Works in July 1984 after signing the Mature Industries bill, which aimed to help the state's industries avoid closing and to assist workers forced into unemployment by closings that did occur. State Representative and Lynn native Timothy Bassett, chair of the Joint Labor and Commerce Committee and a major author of the legislation, stands just behind Dukakis.

In 1982 the Lynnway was lined with car-oriented businesses, most prominent among them dealerships; in 1987 car dealers accounted for $285,717 in sales, by far the largest income of all retail groups. To many the Lynnway by this time was a commercial blight. Just before Christmas of 1977 three Nahant teenagers bombed a twenty-five-foot statue of Paul Bunyan outside the Seacrest Cadillac dealership because, they said, it was "ugly." Photograph courtesy Lynn Daily Evening Item.

However, manufacturing jobs in Massachusetts had declined by only 3 percent in those years, chiefly because the state was in the middle of a business boom generated by the rise of high-technology industry. While employment in the state's textiles, clothing, and leather industries declined 44 percent between 1958 and 1978, high-tech industry employment rose 98 percent. In the early 1980s, as the business boom among these companies continued, GE built its Factory of the Future on Western Avenue in the West Lynn Works complex to develop a model for heavy industry and to demonstrate what efficient manufacturing could be. Yet the company had already begun to cut jobs in many of its factories as military contracts began to decline and commercial air travel ceased to grow. Between 1982 and 1985 the company led the state in the number of jobs lost (4,666), and late in 1991 the company laid off 2,800 workers in Lynn. The Factory of the Future closed in 1996. So did Carr Leather, which had set up shop during the Second World War to process leather and export leather goods and had moved to Lynn by 1969. At about the same time, Henry the

Hatter and Connelly's Candies (founded in 1917), both venerable commercial institutions in the city, also closed their doors.

Clearly, the future of Massachusetts was instead in the continued development of high technology, but the growth of this industry took place outside Lynn. Between 1969 and 1982 high-tech development avoided all of the state's major cities except research-oriented Boston and Cambridge and located instead in the outer suburbs near 128, Massachusetts's technology highway. Communities along Route 128 were home to more than 70 high-tech firms in 1980, but fewer than eight had located in Lynn.

Thus, even as Massachusetts had among the lowest unemployment rates in the nation in the 1980s, unemployment remained relatively high in Lynn. Moreover, like many other of the state's older industrial cities, it was losing both jobs and people. Between 1950 and 1980 the population of Massachusetts grew 23 percent, but Lynn and Cambridge both lost 21 percent of their population, Boston lost 30 percent, and Worcester lost 20 per-

In May 1987 the Lynn chapter of the nationwide Habitat for Humanity program moved a late nineteenth-century house to a new location on Essex Street, where it was rehabilitated and offered as affordable housing.

In 1984 Pollution Control Unlimited installed booms to absorb pollutants at Lynn Beach. Photograph courtesy Lynn Daily Evening Item.

cent. And even as redevelopment and increased immigration caused Boston's population to increase slightly between 1980 and 1986, population in Lynn continued to drop. And the unions in a city well known in the labor movement had also grown weaker: Local 201 of IUE claimed eight thousand members in 1980, half what it had thirty years earlier. In fact the unionized work force had declined precipitously in Massachusetts, much more steeply than it had in the nation as a whole. Between 1984 and 1986 the percentage of the state's work force in unions fell from just less than 24 percent to about 16 percent; in the United States it had declined from just under 19 percent to about 18 percent in those two years.

According to the 1990 census, unemployment in Lynn remained higher than the state average, but the city had clearly made the transition away from manufacturing. Only 22 percent of the

working-age population—7,949 people—held manufacturing jobs. Fully 6,300 of them worked at General Electric, still Lynn's largest employer, while the Boston Machine Works and Prime Manufacturing Company, both making shoe machinery in Lynn since the 1800s, employed others. More than 72 percent of workers were in services, and the city's AtlantiCare Hospital ranked second among local employers with 1,200 on its payroll. In fact, 7,692 Lynners worked in wholesale and retail trade alone, only 257 fewer than worked in the entire local manufacturing sector.

As jobs and population moved to the suburbs or out of the state altogether, Lynn and cities like it in the metropolitan region have watched their property and sales tax bases shrink and their

populations become poorer overall. Median home prices plummeted between 1990 and 1992, from $125,000 to just $87,000, and nearly 60 percent of the housing stock in the city had been built in 1939 or earlier. While nearly 9 percent of Massachusetts families lived below the poverty level in 1990, nearly 16 percent of Lynn families did. In 1990 44.5 percent of the city's people made less than twenty-five thousand dollars a year, and per capita income was only 75.6 percent of the state average. Both the dropout and crime rates were higher than state averages as well.

The statistics paint a bleak picture of modern Lynn, but a few

of them point to a more promising future. Population, for one thing, has been rising since 1986. In 1980, 78,471 people lived in the city; in 1990 Lynn's population stood at 81,245. The city's birth rate in 1991 was above the state average, but so was its death rate, so the trend of population in the future is unclear. Another positive indicator

Lynn Harbor in the 1970s claimed both recreational and commercial activity. In 1973 almost five thousand vessels used it and the Saugus River, and in October 1985 the Lynnway Marina opened for sailboats and private motor craft. In June 1990 Father John Gallagher blessed the city's fleet.

is that construction of single-family homes is also rising: twenty-one permits were issued for them in 1990 while thirty-five were issued in 1992. At the same time, though, multi-family housing permits dropped from twenty-six to zero.

Beyond the statistical indicators are more visible signs of life in the city. The siting of North

In August 1995, Walter Hoey of the Lynn Item *photographed James Runner working with Kristen Shepherd, Jessica Kerns, Meagan Chapman, and Kimberly Luck at LynnArts; at right Caribbean-born Lynners take art classes at the Community Minority Cultural Center in March 1989. LynnArts photograph courtesy* Lynn Daily Evening Item.

Shore Community College on part of the downtown burned over in the 1981 fire brought college students into the area. Work has begun to correct of pollution problems along Lynn Beach, and citizens organized into groups to improve Lynn Woods, High Rock, and other parts of the city. Moreover, compared to many other Massachusetts communities, Lynn reacted promptly to the mandates of the federal Clean Water Act. The city formed the Lynn Water and Sewer Commission in 1982 and secured federal funds to create a new primary wastewater treatment plant (1985), a new water treatment plant (1989), and a new secondary wastewater treatment plant (1990). Federal and state funds covered between 45 and 88 percent of the costs of these facilities, and today Lynn's water and sewer rates are among the lowest on the North Shore, 20 percent lower than the rates communities in the Metropolitan Water Resources Authority pay and 30 percent lower than Boston's.

As the waters of Lynn Harbor improved, the waterfront once again became a desirable public space. One of the two sites of Lynn Urban Heritage State Park is on the waterfront, and in

Founded in 1947, Lynn Ladder has become one of the largest ladder manufacturers in the nation. Here an employee works with one product at the company's South Common Street facility; in 1996 Lynn Ladder purchased the former Coca-Cola bottling plant on Boston Street for use as a warehouse. Photograph courtesy Allan Kline, Lynn Ladder and Scaffolding Company, Inc.

In 1993 David Terry, manager of the market and executive chef at East Coast Seafood in Lynn, displayed a twenty-six-pound lobster for shoppers Elvira Lanzo of Lynn and Marcia Bandoni of Revere. The world's largest distributor of live lobster, East Coast Seafood began business in 1981 and today ships lobster and other seafoods around the globe. It has plants in Lynn, Gloucester, Canada, and Chile. Bob Crosby photograph courtesy Lynn Daily Evening Item.

Basilio Encarnacion prepared a plate of red beans and rice at Rincon Macorisano in March 1995. Walter Hoey photograph courtesy Lynn Daily Evening Item.

1985 a new marina also opened there. The heritage state park has brought new attention to the city's valuable history and historic architecture.

LynnArts, Inc., founded in October 1992, is another vital addition to the city. As the city's community arts organization, it sponsors art, dance, music, storytelling, and other programs for children, adults, and community groups; it also regrants state arts funds to artists, schools, and groups. LynnArts plans to renovate 25 Exchange Street in Central Square, its headquarters since January 1995. Lynn Historical Society, nearly a century old, serves more than four thousand schoolchildren each year and offers a wide range of public programs—walking and bus tours, an annual Halloween outing to Dungeon Rock, historic house tours, exhibitions, and lectures. Moreover, city people have begun a series of activities aimed to prepare Lynn for its sesquicentennial as a city, a year-long celebration scheduled to begin in May 1999.

Moreover, businesses continue to prosper in the city, both new and old ones. Boston Machine Works, founded in 1906, continues to produce machinery for the shoe industry; so does Prime Manufacturing, incorporated in 1927. Barry Manufacturing on Bubier Terrace, which started up dur-

ing the Second World War, still distributes children's shoes around the globe through the Army and Air Force; of similar vintage is Lynn Lumber, now in its third generation of family ownership, and Lynn Ladder and Scaffolding Company, Inc., founded in 1947 and one of the largest ladder manufacturers in the country. Older food processing firms including Boyd's Potato Chips (founded in the 1870s), Durkee-Mower's Marshmallow Fluff (1920), and West Lynn Creamery (1938) have

Lynn children took an active recess break at Lincoln School on September 15, 1987.

Some of Lynn's older markets were revived as well. In July 1995 Renee Maroskos reopened J. Maroskos and Company, a fruit and produce store that had operated in Lynn since 1966; the Maroskos family had been fruit dealers in Lynn for generations. Photograph courtesy Lynn Daily Evening Item.

been joined by newer ventures such as meat company Old Neighborhood (formerly Holiday Brand), and both Gloucester Corporation and East Coast Seafood, which process and distribute scallops, lobster, and other seafood worldwide. Several steel, plastic, machine tool, and other manufacturers continue to produce goods in Lynn, and Zimman's, founded as a dry goods store on Western Avenue in 1935, still conducts a large, regional fabric trade on Market Street, on the site of the former Goddard Brothers department store.

Still, the city's loss of industry and retail trade called for action, and in May 1993 the Lynn Business Partnership, Mayor Patrick J. McManus, and the city council convened the Lynn Summit to begin to form a strategy for improving the business climate in the city, reviving and enhancing the appearance of its downtown, improving public safety and recreational facilities, and developing programs for Lynn youth. Among other things, the Lynn Summit recommended that business development should build on the base of minority-owned businesses that had begun to revive Lynn. A new influx of immigration from the Caribbean has given the city's commercial and cultural life a second wind. In 1950, with the restrictive immigration law of 1924 still in place and the immigrant population in its second and third

generations, 82 percent of the city's population was native-born white. In 1990 the census listed 80.2 percent of the population as white, which includes foreign-born white persons; the population of native-born white now is probably somewhat lower. In 1990 more than 9 percent of Lynners were of Hispanic origin, 6.7 percent were of African origin, and 3.5 percent were classified as Asian or Pacific islanders. In 1995 almost 37 percent of the city's schoolchildren lived in homes where English was not the primary language, and the school system offered bilingual programs in Spanish, Khmer (Cambodian), Russian, Greek, and Vietnamese. One local survey determined that of 2,095 students in Lynn public schools born outside the mainland United States, 33 percent were from the Dominican Republic, 24 percent were from Cambodia (or Cambodian-born children living in refugee camps in Thailand), and 21 percent were from Puerto Rico. There were more than thirty students each from Vietnam, Russia, Haiti, Guatemala, Mexico, and the Philippines. The new immigration has added new ethnic markets, restaurants, and festivals to the city's now-traditional ethnic places and has brought modern Lynn back in some ways to the time before World War I, when foreign-language signs and a panoply of ethnic traditions enlivened city life.

Joe Amaral, general manager Saul Savy, and Mario Pinto work with a hide at Carr Leather in 1984. The company exported light leather goods to Puerto Rico, Canada, and Japan and moved to Lynn in 1969. Photograph courtesy Lynn Daily Evening Item.

Even buildings built after World War II gave way to newer ones. In 1986 the Lynn (originally North Shore) Sports Center on Boston Street, built in 1948–49, was demolished to make space for a new shopping mall.

Current Boston Celtics coach M. L. Carr played a pickup basketball game with Eastern Junior High School students during a visit to the city on November 27, 1990.

Graduates of Lynn Technical High School hammed it up for the camera on June 1, 1990.

Local 201 of IUE led a coalition of unions and community groups in protest against the North American Free Trade Agreement (NAFTA). Workers in an already much depressed economy felt the trade deal would cause the loss of more jobs and a decline in the standard of living. In 1993 Local 201 trustee Stephen "Fuzzy" Herrick (seated) and Local 201 president Jeff Crosby spoke out against the proposed agreement on Western Avenue near Buchanan Bridge.

The twenty-acre Sluice Pond has remained a popular recreation area among Lynners; in 1993 Don Wolf, then twelve years old, was photographed as he concentrated on baiting a hook alongshore.

In 1987 Cambodian residents of Lynn purchased the Calvary Baptist Church on Chestnut Street for its sanctuary, the Cambodian Buddhist Center of Massachusetts.

St. George's Greek Orthodox Church Rev. Charles Mihos, John Mihos, George Nikolakopoulos, and Ted Paragios prepared Greek food for Lynn's Meet Me Downtown festival on Labor Day in 1990.

Students from the Maihos School dressed in Greek costume to celebrate Greek Independence Day on March 25, 1988. Shown here in the front row are Charles John Mihos, Gina Diamantopoulos, and Jimmy Stourvaras; in the rear are Denise Hatzis and Nora Tsoutsis.

Ethnic markets have again
appeared in Lynn as the population
of Caribbean peoples has grown.
Assistant manager Teresa Colon
and owner Agueda Jimenez wait
on Felix Mateo at Jimenez Market
at 199 Union Street in May 1994.
Bob Crosby photograph courtesy
Lynn Daily Evening Item.

In 1991 owner Marie Gaudard
of Vierge Noire Haitian market
in Central Square posed with
a box of imported produce for
newspaper photographer Bob
Crosby. Photograph courtesy
Lynn Daily Evening Item.

The population of Russians has grown steadily in parts of the metropolitan Boston area since political changes unsettled the country
in the 1980s. At Foods of Europe in Lynn, owner Svetlana Groysman
and Natalia Tokarev read the Russian newspaper New Russian
Word. Paula Muller photograph courtesy Lynn Daily Evening Item.

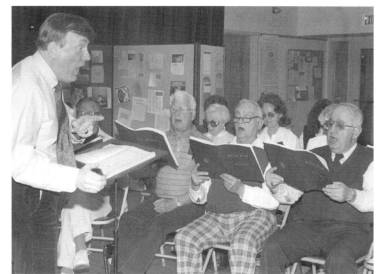

The Concert Singers of Greater Lynn formed in September 1979 to add to the city's cultural offerings. Item photographer Linda Spillane photographed the group in April 1990 as it prepared for one of its twice-yearly performances. William C. Sano, director of the group since 1987, conducts Chet Tilley (partially obscured), Malcolm Dorherin of Lynn, Frank Daniels of Peabody, and Anthony Grappi of Lynn.

In July 1990 Lynn's Jason Bassilakis filled up his car at a gas station on Western Avenue across from General Electric's River Works.

In March 1990 Stan Goldstein switched hats with his father, Lynn's famed Henry the Hatter, by making him try on a few styles.

One of Lynn's most popular retail properties is the sidewalk fruit stand on Broad Street. In 1981 Lynn photographer Peter Bates photographed Mickey Marcus, Dave McLaughlin, and Stan Meltzer at the stand, a summer institution for many years.

In 1985 a crew dissassembled a ten-footer that had stood in back yard of Lynn Historical Society on Green Street and rebuilt it at the visitors center at Lynn Heritage State Park, one of a number of parks Massachusetts helped to create in industrial cities during the decade.

In November 1982, as the Massachusetts Bay Transportation Authority prepared to build its 965-space parking garage, the old Boston and Maine ticket office, an adjoining restaurant, and Dover News were forced to close; the latter two moved to new locations. Boston and Maine sold its passenger service to the MBTA in the 1970s and its freight service to Gilford Transportation Industries, which continues to run freight through Lynn to Salem several times a week. Photograph courtesy Lynn Daily Evening Item.

One of the largest natural parks within the limits of any city in the United States, Lynn Woods had grown shabby and dangerous by the 1980s, and its major entrances were closed off to prevent its abuse by car thieves, drug dealers, drinkers, and motorized vehicles. In 1990, before the park's centennial, Lynners formed Friends of Lynn Woods to begin to reverse the neglect. Dick Hanson, Cecilia Miles, Donna McInerney, and Jack Carroll posed for this promotional photograph before the centennial celebration, organized by Miles and McInerney; all four are General Electric employees. As the condition of Lynn Woods has improved, it has become a mountain biking center for enthusiasts throughout eastern New England.

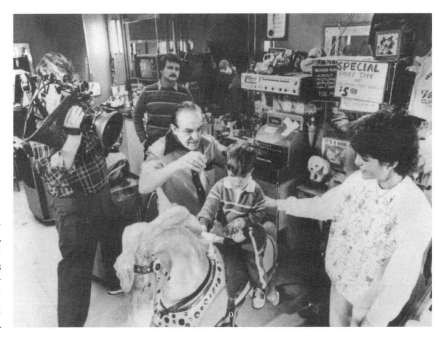

On November 24, 1986, the television show Good Morning, America visited Lynn and filmed two-year-old Andre Pessini as owner Tom Angelucci cut his hair at Vincent's Clip Joint, a local landmark since 1965. Photograph courtesy the Boston Herald.

188

Lynn's Bill Sullivan dressed up as the King on January 3, 1992, the day the Elvis Presley commemorative stamp went on sale at the Lynn Post Office.

During the 1990 Christmas rush owner Tom Mazzaferro shaped a roll of candy canes at Connelly's Candies, which Ed Connelly had begun on Union Street in Lynn in 1917. The firm stayed in the family until 1979, when son Arthur Connelly sold it to Mike and Tom Mazzaferro, who had worked with their parents in Nahant making candy as boys. In 1991 the Mazzaferros sold the company, which had five shops in the region in 1988, to Monica Hollander, and the manufacturing operation was moved to the former Cushman's Bakery plant on Sanderson Avenue in 1993. Bob Crosby photograph courtesy Lynn Daily Evening Item.

As population, jobs, and housing values dwindled, arson struck many of the city's neglected properties beginning in the 1970s. Fires police termed "suspicious" declined from 213 in 1980 to 37 in 1989 but then rose again, with the astronomical increase in bank property foreclosures, in 1990. Item photographer Bob Crosby documented one Lynner's response to the decay on the corner of Orchard and Summer streets in September 1992. Photograph courtesy Lynn Daily Evening Item.

In September 1991 a two-ton truck carrying milk to West Lynn Creamery lost its brakes and crashed through the wall of the J. T. Shawmut restaurant at 155 Boston Street. The driver and the truck were not insured, which delayed work to rebuild the wall. Owner Tom Gandolfo reopened his popular pub on St. Patrick's Day in 1992.

In January 1992 Douglas Allen, longtime Swampscott public official and Lynn insurance agent, stopped in for a shine at Joe Milo's, a shoeshine parlor in Lynn since 1896. Milo, a seventeen-year-old Italian immigrant, had begun the business with a single chair set up outside Hovey's Spa in Central Square. By 1906, with more than thirty chairs, he moved the business to the basement of Basil's Restaurant and by 1944 had moved again to 71 Exchange Street. At midnight on Saturdays, former *Item* editor Vincent O'Brien recalls, the shop was crowded with young men getting shines before church on Sunday. The shop was well known throughout Essex County. Photograph courtesy Lynn Daily Evening Item.

Tish Sterling, manager of Fran's Place on Washington Street, posed for Item *photographer Paula Muller before the bar's HIV/AIDS fundraiser in 1995 for the Lynn Community Health Center and Serving People in Need (SPIN). Fran's Place was originally the Lighthouse, a neighborhood bar that had been frequented by gays and lesbians since World War II. Photograph courtesy Lynn Daily Evening Item.*

In 1985 Rich Viger of Lynn organized a Santa Parade, a December 24 event that now treks a twenty-six-mile path through the city from Austin Square to the Lynngate shopping center. Beginning with only two cars, the Santa Parade now features more than fifty vehicles and lures thousands of spectators. An unidentified Santa tosses candy during the 1986 parade.

Papo Malindez, left, and Tony Sleves spar at Tony Pavone's gym at the Lynn Boys Club.

In 1979 the Community Minority Cultural Center sponsored a float in the city's youth parade; Renee Latimere and Lolitia Moranda worked on it in the Fayette Street yard of Abner Darby. Photograph courtesy Mr. and Mrs. Carleton Brown.

Between September 18 and 20, 1993, local Jehovah's Witnesses completely built a new Kingdom Hall on North Federal Street. With help from fellow Witnesses from nearby states, they completed the job in one day.

In 1982 My Brother's Table opened at 67 Union Street to provide food and shelter to Lynn's homeless; by 1991 the soup kitchen had moved to the city's old post office on Washington Street. Linda Spillane photograph courtesy Lynn Daily Evening Item.

The winter of 1995-96 brought record-breaking snowfall to Massachusetts. After the blizzard of January 9, one unfortunate Lynner on Hollingsworth Street, Dennis MacWilliam, digs out from a garage roof collapse. Photograph courtesy Lynn Daily Evening Item.

In 1995 General Electric in Lynn consisted of one major division—aircraft jet engines—and employed slightly more than five thousand people, a fifth of its peak employment during World War II. At Agganis Square, the company declared obsolete fifteen of the structures at its original West Lynn Works and razed nearly the entire complex except the Factory of the Future. Photograph courtesy Lynn Daily Evening Item.

The Lynn area continues to produce outstanding athletes such as Ken Hill, a pitcher for the Texas Rangers. Other athletes include Chris Howard, also of the Texas Rangers, and Troy Brown of the NBA Atlanta Hawks. In 1996 the Massachusetts Mad Dogs, a professional minor league team, was established in the city with two Lynners, Jay Murphy and Eric Roepsch, on its roster.

On Friday, August 23, 1996, ground was broken for the new home of the Community Minority Cultural Center in the former Empire Store at 298 Union Street. The relocation of the Center from its Sutton Street building is part of a downtown revitalization effort of the Office of Community Development. Participants included, from the left, Rev. Anita Farber Robertson, Rev. Edward L. Green, Virginia Barton, Calvin Young, Elina Mnushkina, E. Carleton Brown, U.S. Rep. Peter Torkildsen, Mayor Patrick J. McManus, Marc Slotnik, Councilor Deborah Smith Walsh, Abner Darby, and Ralph Tyler, Jr.

In 1993 the Wyoma Branch Library was rededicated in honor of Dorothy C. Haywood, chief librarian of the Lynn Public Library from 1956 to 1978. Here, present and former chief librarians Joan Reynolds (left) and Barbara Schaller unveil the new plaque.

Bibliography

In addition to federal and state censuses, regular and special issues of the Lynn *Item*, and the manuscript, scrapbook, and city directory collections at the Lynn Historical Society, the following sources were used in the preparation of this work and may be consulted for information on twentieth-century Lynn:

Betts, William. "Lynn, A City by the Sea." *Outlook* 68 (May 1901): 207.

Billups, Robert, and Phillip Jones. *Labor and Conditions in the Shoe Industry in Massachusetts, 1920–1924*. Washington, D.C.: Government Printing Office, 1925.

Bonislawski, Michael J. "The Anti-Communist Movement and Industrial Unionism: IUE vs. UE." M.A. thesis, University of Massachusetts, Boston, 1992.

Carlsen, Carl. "Life in the Brickyard: Daily Life in a Working Class Neighborhood in Lynn, Mass." Typescript, Lynn Historical Society, n.d.

Carlsen, Carl, ed. *Brickyard Stories: A Neighborhood and Its Traditions*. Lynn, Mass.: North Shore Community College, 1985.

A Century of Progress: The General Electric Story, 1876–1978. Schenectady, N.Y.: Hall of History Foundation, 1981.

City of Lynn, Massachusetts, Semi-Centennial of Incorporation. Lynn, Mass.: printed by the direction of the Celebration Committee, 1900.

The Complete Historical Record of New England's Stricken Area, September 21, 1938. Lynn, Mass.: Daily Evening Item, 1938.

Cumbler, John T. *Working-Class Community in Industrial America: Work, Labor, and Struggle in Two Industrial Cities, 1880–1930*. Westport, Conn.: Greenwood Press, 1979.

Cushing, Elizabeth Hope. *The Lynn Album: A Pictorial History*. Virginia Beach, Va.: The Donning Company, 1990.

Cushing, Elizabeth Hope, ed. *No Race of Imitators: Lynn and Her People, an Anthology*. Lynn, Mass.: Lynn Historical Society, 1992.

Dunning, Robert F. "Wyoma, 1928–1933 (Memories as a Kid)." Typescript, 1989.

Executive Office of Communities and Development, Commonwealth of Massachusetts. "Lynn, Essex County: A Community Profile, 1993."

Farnam, Anne, and Bryant F. Tolles, Jr., eds. *Life and Times in Shoe City: The Shoe Workers of Lynn*. Salem, Mass.: Essex Institute, 1979.

Federal Writers' Project of the Works Progress Administration for the State of Massachusetts. *Massachusetts: A Guide to Its Places and People*. Boston: Houghton Mifflin, 1937.

Giles, Nell. *Punch In, Susie! A Woman's War Factory Diary*. New York: Harper and Brothers, 1943.

Gourley, Meg. "The Rise of Automobility and Dealerships in Lynn, MA." Urban history seminar paper, Northwestern University, March 19, 1993.

Gutman, Richard J. S. *American Diner: Then and Now*. New York: Harper Perennial, 1993.

Lee, Patricia A. "'E Pluribus Unum': The Greeks and Irish: A Comparison of Old and New Immigration with Emphasis on the Ethnic Composition of Lynn." Paper, Salem State College, May 13, 1974.

Liesinger, Diane. "The Lynn Historical Society, 1897–1967." M.A. thesis, State University of New York at Oneonta, 1972.

Lynn Public Library and Lynn Historical Society, *Lynn: One Hundred Years a City*. Lynn, Mass.: Jackson and Phillips, 1950.

Lynn in the World War. Lynn, Mass.: n.p., 1928.

Malm, Finn Theodore. "Local 102, UE-CIO: A Case Study of a Local Industrial Union." Ph.D. diss., Massachusetts Institute of Technology, 1946.

McManus, John A. "The Electrical Industry Comes to Lynn: 75th Anniversary, 1883–1958." Paper presented at General Electric Old-Timers Associates meeting, Thomson Club, Nahant, Mass., August 12, 1958.

Melder, Keith. *Life and Times in Shoe City: The Shoe Workers of Lynn*. Salem, Mass.: Essex Institute, 1979.

Mostow, Stephen G. "Immigrant Entrepreneurs: Jews in the Shoe Trades in Lynn, 1885–1945." Preliminary draft prepared for the North Shore Jewish Historical Society, Marblehead, Mass., August 1982.

Ripley, Charles M. *Life in a Large Manufacturing Plant*. Schenectady, N.Y.: General Electric Publication Bureau, 1919.

Scanlon, Joseph E. "The Day Lynn Burned: November 28, 1981." Typescript, Lynn Historical Society, n.d.

U.S. House of Representatives. *Report of the Industrial Commission*. 56th Cong., 2d Sess., House Doc. No. 495. Washington, D.C.: Government Printing Office, 1901.

U.S. Senate. *Report on Condition of Woman and Child Wage-earners in the United States, 1910–13*. 19 vols. 61st Cong, 2d sess., S. Doc. 645. Washington, D.C.: Government Printing Office, 1910–13.

Upward Bound Oral History/Photography Project. *Voices of a Generation: Growing up in Lynn during the Decline of the Shoe Industry*. Lynn, Mass., 1980.

Van Vorst, Bessie, and Marie Van Vorst. *The Woman Who Toils*. New York: Doubleday, Page, 1903.

Vitale, Richard L. "History of Lynn Harbor Prepared for the Lynn Planning Board." Typescript, Lynn Area Chamber of Commerce, June 1973.

Wetherell, Ellen F. *After the Battle; or, A Lesson from the Lynn Strike: A Word to Trades Unions, Wage Workers, Men and Women, Heads of Families, Mothers of Children, and the Public in General. By a Fellow Worker*. Lynn, Mass.: McCarty, printer, 1903.

Wilkie, Richard W., and Jack Tager, eds. *Historical Atlas of Massachusetts*. Amherst: University of Massachusetts Press, 1991.

Zimmerman, Libby. "Women in the Economy: A Case Study of Lynn, Massachusetts, 1760–1974." Ph.D. diss., Brandeis University, 1977.

200